DRESS UP YOUR HOME!

VERONIKA ZUBKO
OLENA POLKOVSKA

2022

DRESS UP YOUR HOME!

by Veronika Zubko and Olena Polkovska

Originally published in Ukrainian in 2020

Translated from the Ukrainian by Svitlana Kravets

Proofreading by Kevin Custers

Cover and interior design by Bohdana Fomina

Collages by Maryna Sydorenko

© Veronika Zubko, 2023
© Olena Polkovska, 2023

Glagoslav Publications

www.glagoslav.com

ISBN 978-1-914337-78-9

This book is in copyright. No part of this publication may be reproduced, stored in a retrieval system or transmitted in any form or by any means without the prior permission in writing of the publisher, nor be otherwise circulated in any form of binding or cover other than that in which it is published without a similar condition, including this condition, being imposed on the subsequent purchaser.

TABLE OF CONTENTS

- Instead of foreword 6
- Home is where you are: emotions at home and its main formula   9
- It's time to change something: but is it necessary?..................... 13
- 4 Types of perceiving information you should apply to effectively improve the quality of life... 31
- Me in my home: communication and personal boundaries 39
- Touchpoints. Routine vs rituals 43
- Tasks of the house... 47
- Home scents 49
- Eclecticism – a style suitable for everyone 55
- Feng-shui – do I have this in my home? 59
- Entrance hall – the lungs of the house 65
- Baby's room – up to 4 years old 69
- Explorer's room – from 4 to 10-year-olds 73
- Individuality – 11 and older.. 77
- Bedroom: the core of the house. Erotica and nothing more 81
- Bedside cabinets – 27 variations, no classic styles 87

- Bathroom – the skin of your home 91
- Kitchen affairs 95
- Kitchen utensils: quantity and other secrets 101
- Fridge and its contents 107
- One empty shelf 111
- Dining table at which no one sits 113
- A basic set for holidays and table setting exist! 117
- Creative table decoration and broken dishes 123
- Reception and guest room 129
- Workspace or home office 135
- Creative workshop is not a luxury 141
- A place of solitude – a basic need 145
- Living room is the brain of the house 149
- End table and its variations 157
- Tv vs a projector 161
- Sofa and armchairs: no more sets, say yes to accent chairs 167
- #Bringmerugs 175

- Photos in the house 181
- Books and bookshelves in the house 185
- Makeover and decluttering – a permanent process of any cozy home 189
- Plants and flowers 201
- Fresh flowers in the house, or promise to give yourself flowers and this will change your life, #flowersasabasicneed 209
- Collections and collecting: basic level 215
- Art in your home: where to start? 221
- A trip to the flea market, what to focus on 227
- Canonical design items 231
- #Georgecabinet, or start your relationship with retro items 239
- Inspiration for change in your home and how to look for it 243
- Home hacks: unobvious things 255
- Where to do the shopping? 259
- Afterword 273
- Acknowledgments 277

Instead of foreword

Four years ago, in a state of absolute nervous exhaustion and lack of strength, I crossed the threshold of my present home for the first time. I finally saw and realized within it an instrument of my self-awareness. If one could not already see it at such a moment, I indeed would have invented it. Getting to know myself through implementing changes in my home sounded genius.

I remember how my hands were literally itching, and there was finally a light at the end of this depressive tunnel. Oh yes, back then, my home didn't look the way you see it now. It was a long process of getting to know myself and realizing my role in the lives of others. Now I can say three things clearly:

1. With the help of my home and its changes, I became more assertive and more robust and gained the ability to change as soon as I changed my attitude towards it. My home reflects my experience and all the influences others have had on me. I was grateful to my house that it took the brunt of it and helped me with all of the distractions, complexes derived from childhood, sometimes even irritation, and constant struggle with myself.

2. Through working with space in the house, I gained empathy. Now, differently than before, without judgment, I look at other people's

homes: not in terms of beauty but their personal experience. I just said to myself "I have no idea what this person had to go through, why he or she lives a certain way, and what he or she is going through now." I always assumed that, for example, houses littered with clutter often reflect a poor childhood. The pompous style shows the lack of love complexes of people with low self-esteem, seeking the attention of loved ones. Bare and blank walls in apartments devoid of art – maybe people who live there have been taught from childhood that they have to sacrifice themselves; and unwillingness to arrange their everyday life – their protest. Of course, I am not a doctor to diagnose, and the reasons may be completely different; this is just a personal interpretation of the possible causes and courses of events.

3. Then, I became fearless. God, these are just things. They can and should be moved from place to place, donated or sold, and given a new life to. To beat holes in the walls and buy, and then sell unnecessary things. Furnishing your home is a process, and you will need a friend, companion, and guide more than ever. That is why this book was written!

Home is where you are: emotions at home and its main formula

A cozy, abundant home is the way to go. It is getting better every day, but step by step. To make this path a joy, you need to remember three things:

Home is where YOU are.

1. You yourself are primary, your love, taste, charm, and lifestyle. Your family will be happy where you are. That is unconditional love, and you do not have to do anything to the home in order to receive it.
2. Home renovation tells only about financial success and has nothing to do with comfort, taste and style. Therefore, we are surrounded by many expensive but tasteless interiors.
3. Creating a cozy hearth is a fascinating process, first of all, of getting to know oneself: do not rush, do not spoil the "pregnancy". After all, if there weren't 9 months of waiting, there wouldn't be such love after birth.

Perhaps:

- You believe that all you have to do is to save money and hire a designer and it will help you solve all of the problems.
- You have a feeling of emptiness, and you think that you need only furniture / decorations / flower pots for comfort.
- Do you think twice before inviting guests (Will they appreciate your home?).
- You feel dissatisfied with your home and put off housing issues until later.
- You have a strong feeling that the house does not add happiness but adds worries.

Then this is a reason to know that the RESPONSIBILITY for your HOME is YOURS alone.

HOUSE = EMOTION

Its most important formula sounds like:

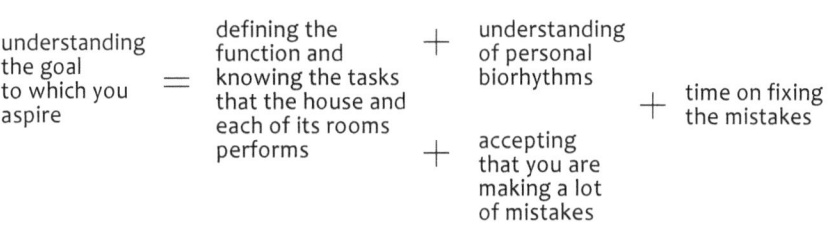

You should remember that a house is a living organism. It reflects your inner world with all its preferences and features. By changing it, you must change yourself.

The home will change, and it isn't possible to make renovation 100 years ahead. You should learn to enjoy the process itself, and you will not have to suffer from the fact that you have not completed something.

It's time to change something: but is it necessary?

Our super-task in the house is to create an interior that over time will find its own unique charm and become only better. Frequently pictures of beautiful interiors have nothing to do with the real life – it is nothing more than a stylistic technique for beautiful photos. On the contrary, comfortable and stylish interiors are often completely uninstagramed.

I can often guess the year in which the renovation was made – people like to use fashionable things and materials, as well as interior solutions that, unfortunately, quickly lose their relevance.

My secret is to use as many untrendy things as possible, and it is advisable to use them so that no one guesses about their manufacturer or store in which you purchased them.

You will find the best things on websites for used furniture sales (you can often find completely new things there), on foreign furniture and décor sites (for this we enter the desired subject in English in the search line and via VPN we change our country into the country of the seller), at all sorts of outlets and stocks. Such things can also be custom made, and handmade.

But let me go back to the beginning.

What is your primary feeling in the house? Ideally, when you're satisfied with 80% percent. The remaining 20% percent will always change, because we remember that a cozy home is a process.

I understand that if you were satisfied with everything at 80% percent, then most likely you would not pay attention to this book. Therefore, if you do read it, you'd probably like to improve your living space a bit, and hopefully set up for a long process. My favorite Japanese wisdom says that fast is actually slow, but every day.

For this reason, I prepared a checklist to find the outdated interior. I suggest going through it and assessing how "outdated" your interior is, and then I will tell you what to do with it.

- ☐ Massive doors and openings / peeling fittings on them.
- ☐ Baseboard – as part of the floor.
- ☐ Net curtains. Curtains with patterns, skimpy, made of unnatural fabrics.
- ☐ Old carpets that were bought not for a specific place, but "for an apartment".
- ☐ Furniture sets.
- ☐ Walls that haven't been painted for a long time.
- ☐ Wallpaper on the walls and wall murals, decorative plaster.
- ☐ No new decor.
- ☐ Old frames in paintings and photographs.
- ☐ Mismatching pots for plants and greenery, which were gifted.
- ☐ Tiles in the bathroom on 100% of the walls.
- ☐ Dim lighting fixtures that are over 7 years old, which give little light or not in the right place.
- ☐ TV opposite the sofa.
- ☐ No zoning but furniture along the wall.
- ☐ Outdated and excess dishes and kitchen utensils.
- ☐ Stretch ceilings and complex hinged structures made of drywall.
- ☐ Linoleum.
- ☐ Old plumbing.
- ☐ Multi-colored textiles in the bedroom, not belonging to a complete towel set in the bathrooms.
- ☐ Forged cornices and window cornices with posh elements.

- ☐ An open space in which odds and ends are stored/shelves with clutter.
- ☐ Outdated light switches.
- ☐ Outdated kitchen fittings and accent kitchen splash back.
- ☐ Obvious joints on the floor, walls, between rooms.
- ☐ A table with massive legs and its complete chairs set.
- ☐ Sliding-door wardrobes.
- ☐ Bulky, massive sofa.
- ☐ Bar counter in the kitchen.

Now we will make an express analysis of these problem areas. I will say right away that they deserve a separate book, and in this one, I want to teach you to see the problem yourself and not to be afraid of solving it.

After all, to make a hundred mistakes = to gain invaluable experience.

Massive doors and openings, peeling fittings on them

Large wooden doors with linings, inserts, veneered blind doors, doors with glass, doors with handles on which the paint has been peeled off or rubbed, doors of a strange, often unnatural color of wood, as well as massive linings and doors that live their own lives. Such doors often draw a lot of attention, "weigh down" the interiors and are often not used for their intended purpose at all.

 SOLUTION:

If such doors are not functional, they can simply be removed. If you need them – that is, when they are functional, are closed and opened daily, and you have the opportunity to replace them – do it immediately. If this is not possible, you can leave the door leaf, hanging it on a barn hanger. Also try painting the doors and/or door trim in the same color as the wall/skirting board or in a contrasting color. Contrasting colors are those that, in the color wheel, are opposite to the existing one. For example, orange, blue and green will contrast to the brown color. To the gray color, it is purple, crimson, yellow and fuchsia. To yellow – turquoise, blue, orange and olive.

> **Important!** To paint doors, choose warm pastel colors. Doors occupy a large amount of room space and it is important that the color is pleasant. Thus, you will significantly "lighten" the color of the door. In an object, it is almost impossible to change the shape, but with the help of color, you can change the perception of the object. When painting, it is easier not to forget to replace the fittings on the door.

Baseboard – as part of the floor

Remember, the baseboard is the foundation of the wall. Most people mistakenly believe that the baseboard refers to the floor, so they often choose it in the same place as the floor. This is a fundamental mistake. The baseboard has nothing to do with the floor.

If you have a narrow strip in the color of the selected flooring; tile baseboard; baseboard with carving; baseboard in color, which is different from the main wall and door; plastic baseboard; with ugly joints, often interrupted connectors, with blaze, with waves; baseboard that lags behind the wall; baseboard with a gap from the wall of more than 0.5 cm and, finally, a plastic baseboard "mimicry of wood" instead of a baseboard – all of them are worth replacing as soon as possible.

The baseboard, although small, is a very important element in your home. It is the lower element of the wall and is very important for the correct visual representation of the living space.

 SOLUTION:

I give you 6 options for the "baseboard issue".
The baseboard should be as simple as possible and high enough (15-20 cm) and painted:
1. Into the color of the door.
2. Into the color of the wall or a tone darker.
3. Into the color of moldings, stucco, window frames

Also, a variant of the baseboard can be:
4. Built-in baseboard, which is invisible.
5. Aluminum overhead baseboard

or:
6. Completely without it (with the right hands of the repair team).

Net curtain

Net curtain – remove and forget about it forever. Throw it out and erase it from your life. It's ugly, it's not fashionable, it's not cozy. If you need tulle in order to hide from neighbors in a block of flats building (and here I've remembered the inhabitants of Copenhagen, with their huge uncovered French windows) – use a translucent material a tone lighter than curtains. My favorite trick is the white and beige linen curtains on the black cornice. Any natural fabric will do.

Curtains with patterns, skimpy, made of unnatural fabrics

Curtains are quite functional: they protect against light and make it possible to produce melatonin in complete darkness, and with them, there is hope for a good sleep, they retain heat and decorate the house.

Keep these three functions in mind when choosing curtains. It is unlikely that lambrequins or bandeau curtains will protect from light, and curtains with a high pickup, like short curtains, will not decorate the house, and, naturally, curtains that like sheet, without a single fold, cover the entire window are unlikely to retain heat. This list should be completed with curtains made of unnatural materials, a loud pattern on them and a large color palette in one curtain.

 SOLUTION:

- Buy ready-made curtains. I think they are the salvation of the budget. I often add some beautiful edgings, decorative finishing,

or wide braids to mass market curtains, and they look quite decent.
- Remember that the curtain rod should at least be wider (20-30 cm) and higher (30-40 cm) than the window opening.
- Use only natural fabrics. Tumbled linen of two colors is a win-win option.
- The pleat of the curtains should be such that when you move them there is a small wave.

Important! You can avoid hanging curtains at all: replacing them with colored wooden shutters, with a roll blackout with a mount on the window frame – are still better than lambrequins.

Old carpets that were bought not for a specific place, but "for an apartment"

Faded, artificial carpets and rugs, high-pile carpets – please give them away.

Carpets themselves are art objects. I love them dearly for being able to visually unite a space. Just choose a carpet that will be of the appropriate size. I remember the cult film "The Big Lebowski" – even its main character understood that without a carpet, the living room looks uncomfortable and unfinished, there is a feeling that something is missing, especially near the sofa and armchairs. Yes, carpets should be cared for, as well as for any piece of furniture in the house.

 SOLUTION:

Read the chapter of this book #bringmecarpets.

Important! Be sure to try on carpets in the finished interior. It is standard practice to order several samples and try them out.

Furniture sets

There is nothing worse than a furniture set. Homes where all pieces of furniture are from one collection do not look beautiful and cozy. It feels like you are in a furniture store or on an exhibition stand. Imagine a girl dressed from head to toes from one store and from the same collection – boring and tasteless, like a fashion magazine model.

 SOLUTION:

Read the chapter of this book "Sofa and armchairs: no furniture sets, 'woohoo!' to accent chairs".

Walls that haven't been painted for a long time

If it seems to you that the Scandinavian white color for the walls and ceiling is the best solution, I dare to object! And if it seems that when you paint the walls in a light color, the room will become larger, the walls themselves will move apart, and the ceiling will become higher, then it just seems so to you. Dark colors will add coziness, and the choice of shades is now so huge that it will be a big mistake not to try them. I will tell you that the Scandinavian white ceiling and walls are only part of the Scandinavian design; in fact, it is very multifaceted.

 SOLUTION:

- Repaint the walls into different colors; choose complex and deep shades. Buy a good multi-component paint, with complex elegant shades. To be honest, this is not easy to find, and it costs more than other paints, but the result is worth it. If you want bright shades that cannot be confused with anything, pay attention to the paint company Decoratorskyi, which is a supplier of paints from leading English manufacturers, and as a result – a conductor of impeccable English style.

- If you prefer natural colors and shades, if you like the Style of Wabi-Sabi, or if there are people with allergies living with you, then choose chalk-based paints (in Ukraine the company Barvaland produces such colors). In the end, don't be afraid to experiment: everything can be repainted. Our grandparents only recently whitewashed the walls twice a year.
- Approach the color issue comprehensively. Not only the walls but also the furniture has a color – it is important to take it into account.
- Consider off-white color options. Such colors are softer and more comfortable; they are better combined with the rest.

Wallpaper on the walls and wall murals, decorative plaster

Wallpaper is probably the main enemy of any space. Remove it and paint the walls. 90% of "renovation respondents" want to replace even modern wallpaper at the end of the renovation.

As for decorative plasters, just remember the Venetian ones – the crown of fashion of the early 2000s. The same will be with the current solutions of wall decoration. If you are not ready to replace them completely in 5-6 years, you should not do it.

 SOLUTION:

Pay attention to dado rails, moldings and friezes, as well as decorative panels: they will never go out of fashion.

Dado rail (chair rails) is a molding line that runs along the perimeter of the room at a certain height and divides the wall into beautiful proportions. Initially, it was used so that dents and abrasions from the backs of chairs did not remain on the walls, and now it is used as an exquisite decorative element. In the classical version, it was at a height of 61 to 183 cm from the floor.

No new decor

Beauty formula: Order + decorate. The most important thing in decorating is that it should be "yours". If you need to consult with someone, then this is not your décor and you should not take it.

 SOLUTION:

Allocate a small and feasible amount of money for decorations each month and buy it gradually.

Old frames in paintings and photographs

Frames in paintings and photographs become hopelessly outdated, so from time to time you need to replace them.

 SOLUTION:

Choose straight black minimalist frames with a white passe-partout, and photos and posters should be glued to PVC and taken in a deep white frame, as gallerists do. And, of course, read the chapter of this book "Photos in the House".

Mismatching pots for plants and greenery, which were gifted

Plants themselves are not decorations. What really works for this purpose is carefully selected pots with flowers in them, in a ratio of 50% to 50%. It is important that the plants bring joy, are healthy and do not clutter up all the empty space. The old saying "If you don't know what to put in the corner, put a flowerpot" is fundamentally wrong. Functionally, plants are to combine space, for example, a sofa and a side table; a chair and a console behind it.

 **SOLUTION:**

Approach the subject of plants comprehensively. There is a whole chapter of this book upcoming: "Plants in the House".

Tiles in the bathroom on 100% of the walls

I recommend tiling only the wet areas of the bathroom and only a minimal amount. Nowadays, many coatings are perfectly washable and can withstand moisture. So in modern bathrooms, there are few tiles. Only leave the tiles where it is really necessary, and be sure to hang a picture on the wall.

 SOLUTION:

If there is an opportunity to get away from tiles, we do it. It is perfectly combined and complements any wall decoration, so that any neighborhood will be appropriate. If a fungus has settled in your home or the tile has acquired a dull shade – feel free to change it to a new one.

> **Important!** The seams on the tile are the object of your close attention, because they can decorate even the simplest tile. And also pay attention to the method of laying tiles – the gold mine of decorators.

Dim lighting fixtures that are over 7 years old, which give little light or not in the right place

Lighting can "stretch" any interior. And even if you have not noticed a lamp without a light bulb for a long time, which has been hanging from the ceiling for many years – this is a trap of the mind: the familiar becomes "invisible".

Dull yellow, old-fashioned chandeliers – this is not about comfort. Lack of light can cause apathy and irritability, this is what the Danes and Swedes tirelessly say – the best manufacturers of lighting, in my opinion.

 SOLUTION:

Change the chandeliers and light bulbs in them. Many excellent options are available in "flea markets" and offered by modern manufacturers. Maybe you can even afford the legendary Artichoke, designed by Paul Henningsen in 1958. Avoid mass trends please: spider chandelier, round ceilings in the style of Tom Dixon, without being the "real Tom Dixon", will very quickly go out of fashion and begin to annoy you.

TV opposite the sofa

Communication, but not entertainment is at the head. TV is one of the ways of spending leisure time, but not the only one.

 SOLUTION:

Turn around the sofa and make it face another sofa or armchair. Feel the difference. Read the chapter of this book "TV vs Projector", and disguise it. Of course, if suddenly you have already purchased a transparent TV by Xiaomi – you can surely skip it.

No zoning but furniture along the wall

 SOLUTION:

In each even small room, you can create at least three zones. How many do you have? To arrange furniture "along the wall" in the living room is not recommended. Move the sofa away from the wall and place a chest of drawers behind it – this technique will give additional space and adds another zone. By the way, the zones themselves in the living room have a functional meaning: for example, a soft zone that consists of sofas and armchairs; coffee area, consisting of armchairs and a coffee table; chess zone, board game area and so on. I will talk more about this in the chapter "The Living Room and Its Inhabitants", and I will touch on this topic a little in the chapter "Sofa and Armchairs".

Outdated, excess dishes and kitchen utensils

Sometimes after purchasing new dishes and appliances, the need for changes disappears by itself. Proper organization of the kitchen is the most important part of a cozy home, which, nevertheless, is able to lead you to a deadlock and make you "roll your eyes" from the scale of the rearrangements.

 SOLUTION:

That is why a whole chapter (even three) devoted to dishes and beautiful servings is waiting for you ahead.

Stretch ceilings and complex hinged structures made of drywall

Nightmare. Just get rid of them and breathe the fresh air. A few of my thoughts to NEVER make a stretch ceiling at home:

- In their manufacture, a chemical film or fabric impregnated with polyurethane is used.
- It's not fashionable at all, but even vulgar and banal.
- Saving the budget is a convention, because it is a direct threat to health.

 SOLUTION:

Just remove the stretch ceilings and advise everyone else to do so also. Destroy strange drywall structures and remove the built-in spotlights from them.

Linoleum

For me, the simplest wooden floor is better than linoleum. I don't think I have to repeat that it disastrously quickly loses its appearance and becomes dull and unattractive.

 SOLUTION:

Absolutely replace it with a more practical and beautiful type of flooring – tile or laminate.

Old plumbing

Every 10 years it is definitely worth replacing, because these are our touchpoints. Everything we touch more than 2 times a day should be the best quality that we can afford. Water quality in Ukraine is far from great, so such a replacement is simply necessary.

 SOLUTION:

Plumbing is an expensive thing that tortures you by limitless choice, but it also hopelessly quickly loses its know-how. Therefore, choose reliable manufacturers and their basic models. They can be found at stocks and at discounts. In addition, if you stop on classic chrome, the choice is always quite large.

Multi-colored textiles in the bedroom, not belonging to a complete towel set in the bathrooms

All you need is two sets for each bed in the apartment. Plain and pleasant to the touch.

 **SOLUTION:**

Calm tones, textile spray, natural materials are the key to your perfect rest. Tumbled linen, washed linen will save time and reduce hassle, because it does not need ironing. The bedspread should be so light that even a child could effortlessly make up the bed. And the bed made up according to the rules should become a natural habit in your home.

Using towel sets is an experience that I borrowed from hotels; it allowed me to qualitatively change the perception of my bathroom. It turned out to be insanely convenient for washing, visually beautiful and collected, very neat and stylish.

 **SOLUTION:**

Start from scratch. Buy the softest, most pleasant to the touch, plain and high-quality towels. For lovers of details – embroider initials on them.

Forged cornices and window cornices with posh elements

The more minimalistic the cornice, the better. A simple matte black cornice with mounting on the wall can be considered universal.

 SOLUTION:

The revelation for me was an electric smart curtains motorized opener – a real pleasure for a hedonist. The remote control is easily programmed for a specific time, so the cornices open and close the curtains themselves. It is convenient when there are many windows in the house, and by pressing just one button, you close / open them all.

An open space in which odds and ends are stored/shelves with clutter

Disassemble such shelves along with the clutter on them; think about storing only the most important things instead.

 SOLUTION:

I will analyze the topic about clutter in details in the chapter "Clutter and uncluttering".

Outdated switches

Switches fade over time and acquire an untidy appearance. This is a relatively painless yet visible way to refresh the space.

 SOLUTION:

Here it is permissible to buy modern, trendy switches. Use their various color and texture solutions in order to emphasize the individuality of the interior.

Kitchen fittings and accent kitchen splash back and counter

These are the most visible signs of an outdated kitchen and, at the same time, one of the easiest ways to renovate it. Where there is a problem, there are always opportunities.

 SOLUTION:

Order new fittings for the old kitchen and emphasize it with a splash back and a countertop. Interesting door handles can be made to order, or ordered on AliExpress. The kitchen splash back can also be changed in a few days without making any repairs. The countertop is a bit more complicated. I suggest choosing concrete, wood or stainless steel – timeless materials that, however, fit both old and modern kitchens equally. They will not contrast brightly with the old facades of the kitchen and will connect the changes in the most harmonious way.

Obvious joints on the floor, walls, between rooms

Such joints are most often found when the flooring material meets another material of the same flooring, with a height difference in the house. For them, there was previously no more understandable way than to close such changes in material with a plastic or wooden strip.

 SOLUTION:

Remove the old strips, ask the foreman about new materials to replace them. Such joints can be replaced with more concise ones (aluminum, copper) or apply the kintsugi technique.

A table with massive legs and its complete chairs set

I have nothing against wooden tables, but often we do not take into account the proportions and size of the room when we buy them. In addition, changing the table is a way to change the space, to lighten it up. Chairs and tables should not be bought from the one set. On the contrary, it will be much better if you replace the chairs from the set:

- with benches, banquettes, on one side of a rectangular table and a set of chairs on the other;
- for round tables you will take different chairs from different eras and countries;
- set of chairs, but not from your set (e.g. model S 33 Tonet).

Sliding-door wardrobes

Today, there is a variety of storage options – from wardrobe systems to nest of shelves. The most important thing here is the transparency of the structures. If there is no way to get rid of them, use Pinterest, there are many different options for remaking them. The goal is to make them invisible.

 SOLUTION:

Use oracal and geometry. Such a cabinet can be reanimated by pasting a large sticker with geometric shapes on its area – squares, rectangles or diamonds. See what this solution looks like here:

Bulky massive sofa

The sofa should not be the visual center of the room, draw the attention away from it.

 SOLUTION:

Read more about choosing a sofa in the chapter: "Sofas and armchairs" and choose sofas on legs.

Bar counter in the kitchen

If you have such a pole, remove it immediately.

The bar table in the apartment is justified if it is a smooth extension of the island, as a space divider and a bar windowsIll table (an excellent solution, by the way).

 SOLUTION:

Without poles, please.

4 types of perception of information you should apply to improve the quality of life effectively

"Just because you can't see something doesn't mean it doesn't exist. And just because you see something doesn't mean it actually exists..."

(Douglas Adams, humorous science fiction novel The Hitchhiker's Guide to the Galaxy)

Psychologists divide people according to the type of their perception into four main groups:

- Visuals (their vision predominates).
- Audials (sounds are important for them).
- Kinesthetics (appreciate tactile sensations).
- Digitals (mind prevails).

All of them differ from each other, for example, in the way they perceive space, and this is very important to know and apply for effective quality of life improvement.

After all, knowing but not doing is like not knowing!

The most common type is kinesthetics (about 40% of the population), followed by visuals (about 30%), then digitals (about 20%) and audials (about 10%).

Let us start with the minority: the audials.

Audials

The direction of gaze of audials is along the midline. The midline is the line of direction of our gaze forward as we sit in an armchair/on a couch/chair. All subjects for the audial should be lined up along this line. If the audial is just building his or her own space, it is important for the architect to give him the opportunity to feel the vibrations and catch the shades of possible sounds: echo, enfilade, high ceilings.

If you are an audial, then your pieces of furniture are:

- Audio systems and speakers throughout the house (there are many design options on sale)
- Automatic curtain closers
- Decorative fountains
- Biofireplaces
- Fireplaces

If possible, the walls should be empty, without pictures – paintings absorb sounds. Instead, you can draw graffiti directly on the wall (or any other kind of wall art).

Digitals

Digitals do not perceive a lot of absolutely amazing and delightful things around.

In the interior, there should be a logical chain, paintings – signs and hidden meanings.

Because the digitals percept the information mainly through logical comprehension, with the help of numbers, signs and logical arguments, they can buy a Miyazaki poster just because they love it. A regular poster will annoy them.

Therefore, simply buying a thing and putting it in the house is not their option.

Digitals will be happy with the things he or she has purchased at the charity fair, UNDERSTANDING the benefits he or she has brought. The digitals' gaze is directed inward. They care about the material and the process of its creation.

Digitals are more focused on meaning, content, importance and functionality.

Suitable for them are:

- Minimalism
- Simple shapes
- Things with history
- Functional things and, vice versa, they need to remove the annoying "just beautiful things"
- Items purchased at charity fairs and auctions
- Multifunctional solutions for their home
- Natural materials
- Experimental materials and objects
- Collections of anything

Visuals

For visuals, everything should be BEAUTIFUL! Visuals are ready to buy something spectacular and bright for the house, even if it is uncomfortable.

Therefore, all object design is their weak point.

When communicating, visuals direct their gaze mainly upwards.

Therefore, it is important for visuals to pay attention to chandeliers and lighting fixtures, they will like the unexpected color of the ceiling, ceiling rosettes and bas-reliefs.

From art: graphics, charts (topographic maps) and photographs are suitable.

Visuals regularly visit picture and photo galleries. Colors, their combinations, shades and shadows are very important for them.

Their choice:

- Photos and graphics of large sizes
- Colored ceiling (color blocking)
- Greenery (flowerpots) in the house
- Ceramics in natural colors
- Sculpture
- Contemporary art
- Colored dishes in the kitchen
- Books in colorful covers (interior or coffee table books)

Kinesthetics

Kinesthetics (tactile) "feel" the world around them and perceive most of the information through bodily sensations: smell, touch, with the help of movements, etc. Comfortable furniture is important for them, along the contour of which it is pleasant to move their hand; materials should be soft and velvety.

The house should smell good. Kinesthetics need to move and taste, touch, feel, and smell everything.

They need:

- Leather sofa with velvet pillows
- Macramé
- Hemp or faux fur
- Indian carpets

- Cashmere plaids
- Faience and porcelain
- Oil paintings
- Natural wooden table
- Natural linen
- Diffusers
- Silver appliances
- Library
- Hardwood floor

Kinesthetics do not know how to hide their feelings; their eyes betray them. Therefore, they often lower them. That's why floor is the first thing they need to "upgrade" in a new place. For them, the floor and the material, which it is made of, are extremely important. They will like the oak parquet, board and all the materials that are pleasant to the touch. They often walk around without slippers and do not understand why someone needs them, and the best gift for them is an electric broom.

Kinesthetics are people of action.

It is important for them to make rearrangements, so they need to avoid massive built-in furniture pieces.

The kinesthetic remembers the overall impression.

Humans have 5 senses:

- Sight
- Hearing
- Taste
- Smell
- Touch

Important! The more sensory organs are involved in the objects of everyday home use, the more such an object is "timeless" and the more it will please you.

Your task is to choose those things that affect not one, just several of the senses.

Thus, when choosing your bedding – pay attention not only to its tactility and materials. Let its color be soothing, and on the shelf where it is stored, put a bag of lavender or sandalwood and add a little starch to the wash – and then it will crisp as gently as in the most expensive hotels.

I am a tactile to the core, so Bali-style silk robes are something I love to wear. But silk is not the only important thing, because in such bathrobes there is a fairly large variety of author's prints – so I visually get pleasure, and I can also sprinkle them with a textile spray, and now my item has already involved three sense organs.

A home is for all the senses, we all love them, we need them all, and do not forget about any of them – this is the main formula of this chapter.

Homework:

1. Determine your type of perception of information. There may be several of them in different ratios.
2. Make a list of what could be improved for your type of perception.

Me in my home: communication and personal boundaries

The keystone. Basis.

The freedom to wave your arms ends where another person's nose begins. To defend your boundaries (without which, by the way, you can't live a happy life) without respect for others is ridiculous.

The responsibility for our home lies on us.

Do you remember the three most important points in the first chapter?

Our loved ones feel good with us in any home; its decoration is only our choice. Therefore, Cinderella syndrome ("a fairy will come and do everything for me") and the sacrificial position are our worst enemies.

There is a checklist ahead to check the violation of these very boundaries in the home:

- ☐ no place of privacy / hours for privacy;
- ☐ the home does not reflect the interests of all those living in it;
- ☐ there are no locks on the doors (except for common areas, but sometimes I welcome the lock on the refrigerator);
- ☐ in no room (including the nursery!) there are closed shelves / storage places with a lock;
- ☐ the rules of the home are not written down or no one knows them;
- ☐ you have an inferiority complex in the home, especially if it's not yours.

My home is me

I am the beginning; I am the most beautiful and most valuable object in my home. Nothing will replace me, for I can breathe life into any room.

My soul, my self-expression, and everything I create in it, be it love, children or vases, are the components of this very home.

It is good if you live in a big house. Everyone has their own room and there is a common area for joint activities. But you can also live happily in a one-bedroom apartment! Even if you live with relatives, and legally they have the right to the premises, you still have the right to your personal boundaries. You ask me: "Decor, interior and... boundaries? Boundaries are psychology!"

The good news is that we are going to sort them out now.

Firstly, only you are responsible for the comfort inside the home! No one should share this desire with you. You do it for yourself. Not for your husband, not for your children, nor for the guests and relatives. A pleasant side effect will be the realization that this will change their world too. But only after yours. It's your choice, and they don't have to share it.

What you can do to set boundaries:

Step 1.
Tell the family members what you INTEND to do. Tell them why this is important to you AND OFFER them to join you. Tell about clutter and

its effect on life. Picture it in emotions, how you want to feel in your home.

Step 2.
Avoid the phrases "it will no longer be as before", "we will change forever". Actions speak louder than words! Don't scare others and yourself.

Step 3.
Create a place for privacy / designate hours for privacy.

Not only for yourself, but also for the family members. If there is a separate room, it is ideal. If not, it might just be a place for privacy. At least 20 minutes in any place just for you, when other family members are strictly forbidden to enter. This is important for kids too! They understand what personal boundaries are and will build their own.

Step 4.
Offer to help:
"What can I do to make you feel comfortable?"
"What do you lack to organize the space?"
"Do you need help cleaning up?"

Step 5.
House rules.
I remember Harlan in the film "Knives Out" and his mug with the sacramental "My House, My Rules, My Coffee" – this is a truly hedonistic position.
Do you have any rules? No? It's time to come up with them.

Step 6.
Check the feedback from the family members a month later, be sure to mention in advance the date of the conversation. Ask how they feel, whether they like the changes, what good or bad it has brought them, whether they are ready to continue.

My home is me. I respect myself and know my boundaries. But I also respect the boundaries of others, even the youngest members of the family.

TOUCHPOINTS.
Routine vs rituals

A routine is everything we do on a daily basis. These could be getting ready for work in the morning, our daily habits, cleaning the house, etc. Basically everything our life consists of.

There are morning and evening routines, routines for taking care of the children, for yourself, to bring order in the house, and many others. It is good if you know your routines – they will help you to be more efficient and collected, and as a result – calmer and more confident. However, I know a way that, in my personal opinion, can make you even happier! If I would have to describe the whole concept briefly, then:

Routine takes energy, but rituals produce it

You can turn routine into rituals with the help of design and high-quality things, as well as things that you really, really like.

The so-called points of touch, of frequent use, points of contact with physical objects on your daily basis, a.k.a. TOUCHPOINTS.

> **Remember!** What you touch more than 3-4 times a day should be of the highest quality you can afford.

To give yourself much more than money – to pay attention to yourself: this is the new luxury of our days.

As the topic of morning rituals and their beneficial effects on us is covered in separate books, for example "The Miracle Morning" by Hal Elrod and others, I will not raise this topic.

I won't consider the rituals themselves, but the practical things that you will need for them.

Attention! If you consciously "touch" something with your eyes (during watering houseplants, for example) – this is also counted as a TOUCHPOINT.

Look at this checklist and see whether you need to improve the quality of your TOUCHPOINTS.

If we consider the average person and his or her habits in the context of working days, the list will be approximately as follows:

- ☐ Bed linen and pillows
- ☐ Pajamas
- ☐ Bathrobe and the place where you take it from
- ☐ Slippers
- ☐ Pots / watering cans
- ☐ A glass of water and a carafe
- ☐ Vase
- ☐ Knives
- ☐ Kettle
- ☐ Notepad and pen
- ☐ Perfumes
- ☐ Scented candles
- ☐ Bedside mat
- ☐ Towels
- ☐ Toothbrush
- ☐ Yoga mat
- ☐ Plates
- ☐ Teapot
- ☐ Soap
- ☐ Coffee/teacup
- ☐ Home clothes
- ☐ Fabric shaver
- ☐ Electric broom
- ☐ Night light or bedside lamp
- ☐ Phone charger

The list is approximate; you will have your own personal TOUCHPOINTS. It is important to surround yourself with the best possible things, as these routines make up 80 percent of our lives. Now it is a good time to slow down and pay attention to them.

Homework:

1. Make a list of things you touch more than 3-4 times per day.
2. Create a folder "Touchpoints" on Pinterest and include the items you dream of.

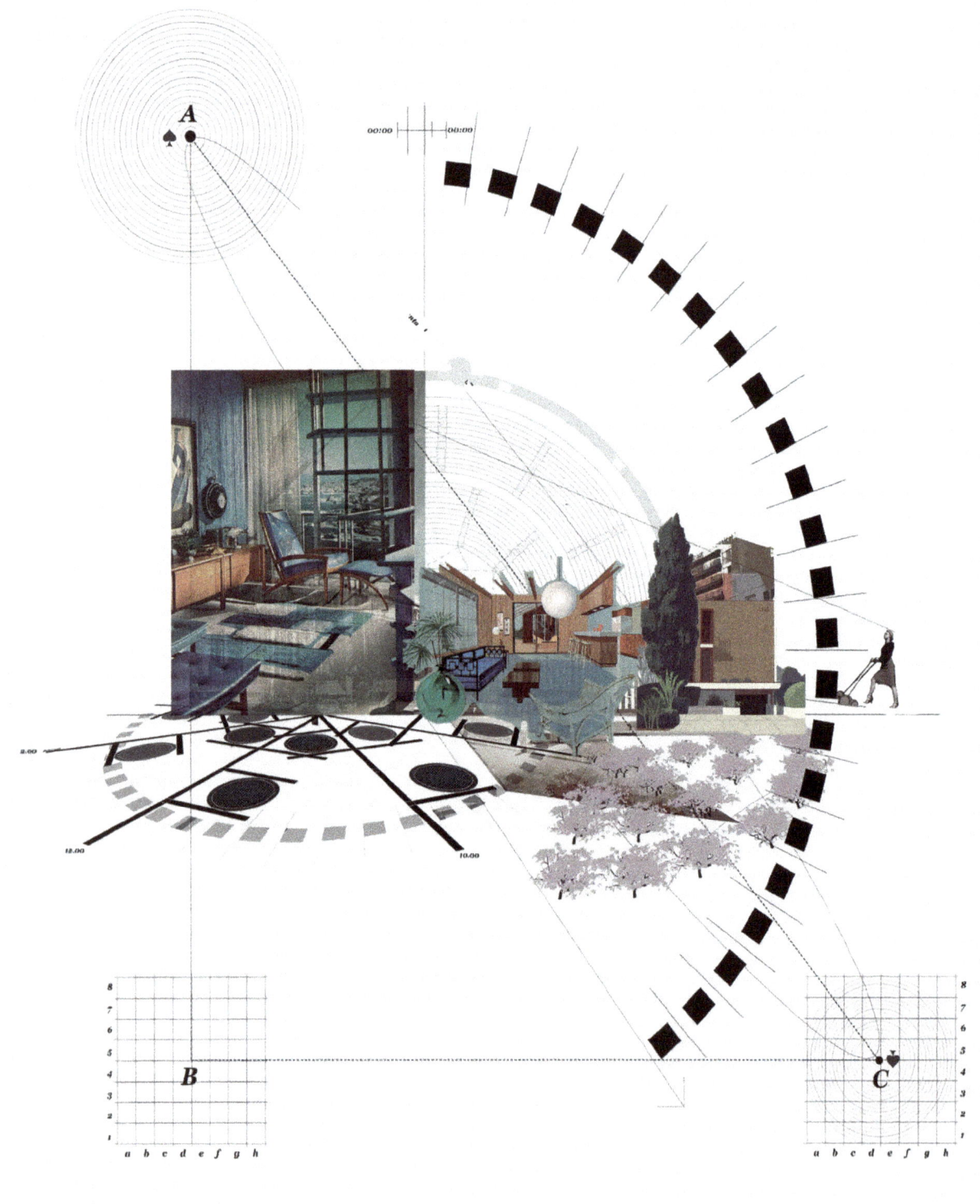

Tasks of the house

If we talk about the interior, then given the reality of our fast-moving life and the pace at which everything is happening now, the house must perform several tasks.

Tasks of the house:

- To clear and stabilize

In no case should the house burden you with things. It should not make you think "this must change, this is to be repaired, and this should be moved." Everything should be clear, simple, favored and functional.

- To fill

The house should fill you with a sense of pride of yourself, gratitude to yourself – for the fact that you are such a great person. While someone else was waiting for Monday, you slowly and surely were creating your dream home. It does not matter whether it is your own apartment or rented housing; how much time you spend there and with whom you share it. Still, your home should fill you with a sense of gratitude for loved ones, a sense of admiration, a joyful expectation of tomorrow.

- To meet the basic needs such as food, sleep, cleanliness

- Be a spiritual guide

This is just about personification. Why collect something if you're not going to keep it in the most prominent place? Or why buy a beautiful tablecloth if you use it once a year? There are plenty of things that can turn your regular meal into a gourmet dinner and the bathroom into a spa. It's all available now, and it's important to understand what's really important to you in the house.

- The house should be flexible and capable of change

You change, and the house has to correspond to your changes. If you return to the place of your strength in 6 years, you will understand that something is wrong there: you have changed, but the place, unfortunately, has not.

Home scents

"If you turn your nose away from the scent of your home, then it's not your home."

Chris Riddell

The smell in the house consists of:

- furniture and its smell
- household chemicals that we use
- smell from the refrigerator
- humidifiers
- dry herbs
- aroma candles
- diffusers
- aroma lamps with open fire
- Berger lamps
- flowers
- houseplants
- scented sachets
- perfumes for the house
- the smell of pets

Remember: home = emotion.
The smell always evokes emotions.

Furniture. I buy old furniture only if it doesn't smell. Restorers often know how to get rid of it, and then the thing easily settles in my house. Smell the new furniture. Its manufacturers often use toxic materials. Leather with improper manufacturing technology also has an unpleasant odor. All furniture made of wood is exceptionally fragrant. All the oils for its care are just wonderful. In general, by the way, furniture care is a habit that should be instilled.

Household chemicals are your enemies when it comes to "smells in the house". Use fragrance-free cleaning products. I use of the DelaMark line; they have a wide range of home care products and fragrance-free household chemicals.

Refrigerator. Nothing spoils the impression of the house more than the unpleasant smell from the refrigerator, to which the owners of the house sent you for ice or mint.

Tip: use odor absorbers and remember: inside should be more beautiful than outside! Therefore, please check the expiration dates of sauces and other jars in it at least once a month.

Dry herbs in vases are the most proven way to aromatize bathrooms, bedrooms, pantries, hallways and utility rooms.

What else is that? Right, childhood! That is the reminiscent of grandma's attic smell.

The smell of **Aroma candles** is the only smell that doesn't have to correspond to the general concept of the house. Keep a few aroma candles at home and create the atmosphere in which you want to be.

Romantic amber, exciting musk, refreshing invigorating fresh citrus or New Year's spices – cinnamon, cardamom, saffron. The smell of cigars, freshly ground coffee or freshly baked bread, the smell of books and the library – all this is available to you for every evening.

Home scent diffusers/perfumes.

The mistake is that we often confuse them with air fresheners, although diffusers are the main smell of the house, which the more constant, the better.

Such smell is basic and should be felt in every room. The basic smell is like underwear, you wear it all the time.

Similarly, on top of the main basic smell, you "put on" an aroma candle, textile sprays and so on. But, underwear is always on you. Well, almost.

Flowers

The scent of flowers is the very aroma of a neat and caring house. As you remember, flowers are a basic human need.

In a separate chapter, I will tell you how their presence in the house can change everything.

Houseplants smell too. Olive trees, jasmine, citrus fruits, heather and lavender are your most cherished helpers in cleaning the house and filling it with aroma.

Now it's time to talk about the little secrets in all my closed drawers. In all these boxes, I keep bags of dry herbs or **scented sachets**.

There is nothing more pleasant than opening the shelf at the bottom of the desk in search of a pen, stopping for a second, inhaling the smell of lavender or bergamot.

Tip: instead of scented sachets, you can use unwrapped mini-soap of famous perfume brands, such as you can find in hotels. Wax soap of perfume houses is a confirmation of this.

Textile spray (in support of morning rituals).

Spray it slightly on your bed linen or towels before storing them in a closet.

The Lampe Berger are my recent and favorite revelation – it not only scents the air in the room, but also purifies it.

The Lampe Berger was invented by Parisian apothecary Maurice Bergér more than 120 years ago. Initially, it was intended for disinfecting the air in hospitals. Later, aromatization was added to the function of disinfection, and the bottles of lamps began to be made in collaboration with famous French designers and manufacturers.

Today Maison Berger Paris offers a great variety of models of lamps and aromas, but most importantly – clean air in your house. It takes only 20 minutes of the lamp to destroy 68% of the microbes and bacteria present in the air and to fill the house with exquisite French aroma. It is also interesting that, unlike other types of aromatization, the Berger lamp does not just mask unpleasant smells but destroys them at the molecular level.

Humidifiers with a couple of drops of aromatic oils can humidify the air, soothe and tune in to a good sleep.

When choosing a particular smell, I always look at the environmental friendliness of the brand and its packaging, choosing only those that I can reuse as a decoration.

Here is a list of brands I love:

- **MUJI** are the best humidifiers I have come across: small, inconspicuous and minimalistic. They also sell aromatic oils for them.

- **Jo Malone** – home aroma diffusers. They are interesting because the smells can be mixed, creating unique combinations.
- **Gunja** – I love their ceramic vases, which can be used for small things like rings on the bedside table.
- **SISTER'S AROMA** is a Ukrainian brand of fragrances for all intents and purposes, including the car. I dearly love their home summer scents – because they combined the orange and cherry blossoms with a soft cashmere finale.
- **Diptyque** – aesthetically perfect fragrances, especially their scented ovals on the textile strap and perfumed body stickers are incredible.
- **WOOD MOOD** – incredible clean candles of Ukrainian production and pride of the nation, which I am not afraid to overestimate with such words. Instead of a container for their incredible candles, they use burnt wood – a real find for decorators, and their candle with hand embroidery is the best gift without a reason.
- **Laurel Home** is a Ukrainian brand that pays attention to details. Their unique products are aroma stones and aroma sachets. For me at one time it was a discovery of such a sachet bed linen storing cabinet. Since then, I have been constantly using this life hack.
- **Lothantique** is the best textile spray with a large selection of incredible fragrances.
- **Diwali candles** are candles made of soy wax, with scents of American branded essential oils. My favorite Norwegian Wood and Cinnamon Rolls fill the room with a natural smell in half an hour.
- Collaboration **IKEA*Byredo**. 13 crazy fragrances that can excite emotions: nostalgia, ambition, intuition and comfort!

Eclecticism – a style suitable for everyone

Eclecticism is suitable for everyone.

The formula of our chapter is as follows:

$$\text{DECORATION / DESIGN} = \text{PERSONIFICATION} + \text{COMFORT}$$

$$\text{PERSONIFICATION} = \text{your feeling today} + \text{the relevance of your space – unnecessary things}$$

Your feeling today is a variable position, so there is no permanent solution to this equation.

We can only create a beneficial base.

Why eclecticism? It is the only style suitable for everyone. We all perform many roles, living many lives.

We feel good in a house with one style in one role, and completely uncomfortable in the same style, but in a different role.

Weekends and weekdays, vacation time, quarantine and holiday time also look different.

Our main goal is to create many zones / islands for all our roles.

Do you remember the chapter on TOUCHPOINTS?

Historically, a person has been able to do one thing really, really well. Both in fashion and in the manufacture of furniture and other things, craftsmen passed on knowledge and skills from generation to generation.

In order to create eclecticism and surround ourselves with the best things, we can take the best product from each nation + not forget about self-identification (your own nation or several, if you live in a multinational family) + stick to the percentage (below):

$$\text{ECLECTICISM} = \frac{\text{the best product from each nation} + \text{products of self-identification}}{\text{percentage of eclecticism in objects}}$$

I can say that avid travelers can show off their own large and diverse collections, brought from everywhere, but meanwhile I'll offer you a personal shopping list from different countries. Thanks to the Internet and language skills, we can buy anything anywhere, and it is incredibly inspiring.

So, what and where I buy:

- Carpets: Turkey, India, Georgia, Morocco
- Object design: Scandinavian countries
- Care products: England, Japan, Asian countries
- Equipment: Italy, the USA, Germany
- Art: Berlin, London, Ukraine
- Antiques: Belgium, France, Estonia, Netherlands
- Furniture: Denmark, Finland, the USA
- Tableware: France and England
- Interior books: England, Germany
- Handmade: Ukraine, Iceland, Australia, Finland
- Textile: Italy, Austria, Belgium, India
- Ceramics: Israel, Czech Republic
- Scent: Ukraine, France

The percentage of eclecticism includes:

- Vintage (10-20%)
- Object design (10-20%)
- New things of modern production (40%)
- Handmade (20%)

It should be noted that at least one third of the items on this list must be art objects or limited issues, i.e. unique.

Once you have the basic and simple formula in your pocket, don't be afraid to add something of your own and experiment.

Feng-Shui – do I have this in my home?

Probably many of you have heard such terms as "Feng Shui", "Yin" and "Yang", "Qi" and "Sha", and some of you probably think it's from the realm of magic, religion, or superstition. In fact, it is a science, which is quite serious and profound, aimed at achieving a positive impact of space (read: your home) on the people who occupy it (i.e. you).

Since this book is about the home, the place where you live, recharge, get inspired and simply relax, I think it is necessary to reveal to you the basic rules / secrets / concepts of Feng Shui, so that your home is not just a simple place, but also a place of strength and joy for you.

Therefore, to make your home a place of strength, it must meet four important criteria:

- be in a good place, pleasant for living – with easy access from the road, away from busy street traffic, must have an open space – the front yard;
- it must have a holistic form with a complete and attractive appearance, since holistic forms reflect holistic energy, while fragmentary and irregular ones enhance chaotic energy;
- it must have a smooth flow of Qi (life energy) – the movement of energy within the home must not be too fast or too slow. If the rooms, corridors, and passages have a good connection, then the residents will build a good relationship with each other;
- to evoke good feelings – people immediately feel the places where they are comfortable and where they are uncomfortable, this is our natural reaction to the energy of the space of the house. If you pay attention to it, it will become clear in which place it is favorable and in which it is not.

More often than not, an apartment, much less a house, has a living room, bedroom, kitchen, bathroom, closet, and probably many other useful (and not so useful) rooms. But the main entrance, bedroom and kitchen are the three most important "players" of the house or apartment. Therefore, after becoming more familiar with them, you will definitely progress in finding the G-spot of your house!

Feng Shui Entrance

Remember: the front door is like a human's face; through it you look at the world, and the world gets to know you. It reflects the personality and character of the house, as well as it's the main entry point of good energy to you.

Every time you walk through a "good" door, you activate success and strengthen your home, and it already certainly supports and protects its inhabitants. Therefore, it is extremely important that nothing obstructs the entrance and the flow of good energy from outside goes smoothly into your home and evenly fills the entire space.

Take care that the place of passage right behind the front door is simple and pleasant, not cluttered and cramped. Clutter in the apartment in general clogs the energy, but especially so if it is at the entrance. It is preferable to equip entry hall with lockers and shelves where you can store shoes, outerwear, umbrellas, etc. Aside from general good energy, you and your guests will definitely also like to be welcomed by green plants at the entrance. The room should also be well lit and have a pleasant aroma.

The most important place in the house according to Feng Shui

The bedroom is one of the most important places in the house, because that is where we spend a third of our lives. Feng Shui of the bedroom affects all aspects of life, especially health, relationships, and emotions.

The main purpose of a bedroom is to relax, to refresh, and to restore our energy. That is why it should be calm, cozy, comfortable, and not too big so we can always have enough energy in it. There should not be too many windows, too much light, or overly bright colors in the bedroom.

The most important thing in the bedroom is the location of the bed:

- its headboard should be at a blank wall, behind or above it there should not be windows and openings, because it is a support in life;
- the door or passage should not be located in the same wall as the headboard;
- the bed should not be placed opposite the door;
- it is better to place the bed so that the door or passage was diagonal and viewed when you lie in bed;
- directly above the bed there should not be beams, kinked ceiling, or any heavy objects. Chandeliers should be moved as well;
- you should not place any storage space under the bed, as this may cause financial or even health problems;
- a mirror opposite the bed might also cause bad dreams, health problems, and relationship problems;
- in general, if there is a blank wall behind the headboard, and there is enough space and air in the bedroom, you are likely to have a good sleep and good health.

The perfect kitchen according to Feng Shui

We all spend a lot of time in the kitchen. This is the place where we cook, eat, chat and do other important things, and in the meantime, it all affects our health, family relationships as well as the family budget.

The two most important elements in the kitchen are the stove (fire) and the sink (water), so it is extremely important that they do not "look" at each other, because these two elements are not very friendly. The names of the elements are metaphors for feminine and masculine energies, so opposing energies can worsen the relationship between man and woman in the home.

The ideal placement of the stove and the sink is at a 90-degree angle to each other, with the sink by the window and the stove by the wall. The stove symbolizes fire and is associated with spending money, so the wall behind the stove will provide support and control, meaning the family will have stability and budget under control. If there is no possibility to create a 90-degree angle, then the sink and stove should be placed on the same line, you can place them next to each other.

The arrangement of the refrigerator, microwave, and other kitchen appliances is a secondary issue. It's important to take care of the main players. If the stove and the sink are placed correctly, ordering everything else in the kitchen is not difficult: place them where it is convenient and ergonomic.

Entrance hall – the lungs of the house

I am convinced that every space in the house has its own function and should be filled accordingly.

So, what should the entrance hall "do":

- Greet those who come in, say that they are welcomed and loved;
- Store outer garments and shoes;
- Store care products for outer garments and shoes;
- Store and timely offer essentials: perfume, lipstick, keys, etc.;
- Give you the opportunity to look at yourself when you leave the house;
- Set you up for a new day when you leave the house, and for the comfort of home when you return;
- Allow you to dress comfortably and take off your outerwear and shoes;
- Fill you with joy.

In short, the two main functions of the entry hall are storage and emotion.

The entry hall serves as the lungs of the house. Let them be clean and breathe freely.

Checklist for shopping for the entry hall:

- ☐ A vase with flowers, herbs or branches. If space is limited, look for a vase for one flower. In the vase-flower duo, one of them should be of unusual shape. Therefore, the entry hall is a great place for vases of unusual shapes and colors;

- ☐ Houseplants. Pick them up for the pots. Pots for plants made of copper or brass look especially cozy. You can find them in 🅖 marmur.studio. Tip: an ice bucket with mascarons is a great alternative to pots;

- ☐ A sculpture. It should be small and be the leitmotif of a flower arrangement in a flowerpot;

- ☐ Paintings, posters and photos. It would be great to place such art in the entry hall with a bit of humor or written slogans, for example: "My house. My rules. My coffee" or "Be amazing today". A nice selection of art photos that will prove you are a person with good taste and sense of humor you can find at 🅖 olha_stepanian, 🅖 colored.phenomena, 🅖 lilit_artstore, 🅖 mitskevich_co, 🅖 stuzha_store;

- ☐ A chair, a bench or a pouffe. Since the furniture in the entry hall is often built-in, a chair, a bench or a pouffe may be the only item that can attract attention. It is important for it to not be oversized and it must be easily movable. This allows you to easily change the space and simplifies cleaning. Pay attention to the benches of 🅖 buro150 and 🅖 woodwerk_ua. And you can add an accent on your chair if you paint it with bright Decoratorskyi paints;

- ☐ Dresser console. When there is little space in the entry hall, the area of the upper part of the shoe cabinet from IKEA STYLE can serve as a console. Just as we need air, we also need a horizontal surface in the hallway for convenience and storage;

- ☐ Mat. Choose mats of unobtrusive colors and without a pattern. Family logo may be an exception. A good solution is to buy mats in pairs and place them on both sides of the door;

- ☐ Mirror;

- ☐ Storage cabinet. I highly recommend thinking through the ergonomics of the cabinet, so as not to lose space. As a rule, there is not too much space in the entry hall, and up to 40% of the usable space is lost because of improperly organized cabinets. This is exactly the 40% that is needed for cleanliness and order in the entry hall;

- ☐ A hanger at the entrance is a guarantee of a place to hang your bag. It is good to have separate bag hooks for each member of the family;

- ☐ Organizers: baskets, boxes, plates for tiny items. Storage is the basis of orderliness, but order is not more important than beauty. And you don't necessarily have to sacrifice style and beauty to achieve it either;

- ☐ Sunglasses holders. A necessary thing as a sunglasses holder will be very convenient at the exit. It is better to hang it on the wall so as not to occupy horizontal surfaces. There is an interesting solution in 📷 the.art.room.ceramics, where holders for the glasses are the ceramic noses;

- ☐ A place for keys. They can be put, hung, thrown, but the main thing is to provide a place for them! Vintage trays from 📷 shabby.store are universal for storing any trinkets.

The entry hall should be darker and richer than other rooms in the house. Do it, finally.

Baby's room – up to 4 years

If you're lucky enough to have a separate room, the baby needs a purely functional space, convenient for both the baby and the adult:

- for sleeping
- for games
- for changing clothes

At this age, the baby usually stays with adults. Therefore, the room should also be convenient for adults.

Checklist for this room:

- ☐ air purifier
- ☐ humidifier
- ☐ nightlight
- ☐ large armchair with a footrest for feeding the baby or for a rest
- ☐ rug
- ☐ crib
- ☐ changing table
- ☐ wardrobe
- ☐ abstraction paintings of large size
- ☐ area for the development of fine motor skills
- ☐ flowerpots with greenery

This list should be considered with due care. It is important that things are of good quality, so that their appearance does not deteriorate from use and can easily be reused by future brothers or sisters. In addition, the models of leading manufacturers are so classic and do not change from year to year, that you can easily sell them while maintaining the reuse principle. And most importantly, in the leading manufacturers of kid's products: all products are tested and certified, so when choosing a store for kid's products, look for the official representatives in multi-brand stores. In such a room, it is also good to have a large schedule with the baby's daily routine and a memory board, on which you will stick the baby's photos – children grow very fast. The room for the baby is a place to experiment with, so feel free to add textures and colors. With Barvaland eco-friendly paints, this can be done safely and very quickly, so you can "redo the room" or just "change the bed" while the child is out for a walk, and such a redesign will definitely be useful.

Homework:

Describe the so-called "clients way" in the baby's room: what you and your baby usually do and where you usually are. Think about and provide your comfort in these areas.

Explorer's room – from 4 to 10 years old

I deliberately deviated from the phrase "children's room" in the title. Firstly, forget that word, I beg you!

It diminishes the possibilities. Don't you think so? The word itself. There are no "children's rooms". There is your child's room. The room of a big (not a small) personality. For their exploration. For their discoveries. For their dreams. For the most relevant issues.

As well as to every person, basic functions are also important to a child in his or her room: sleep, time for oneself and creativity.

First of all – the organisation of these functions. And then – a blank canvas. Gender-neutral room. Organic chaos. Let it be filled and changed by the child. Let it "grow up" along with your kid. This is his or her room, not yours. Mum! Stop stuffing it with all your whims, leave alone Pinterest and references, go back to your room!

Well ok. Let's leave this room for future home investments.

Yes, if the child is small, they will definitely need a crib and a chair for mum. That's what the previous chapter of the book was about.

And the organisation of toys. Even in this case, only as a last resort should you interfere with their business. Let the child understand that arranging its own toys is an amazing opportunity for creativity. Believe me, your child will quickly realise that an uncluttered room is much more comfortable to live in!

Just stop looking for a pink crib and a mint bedding!

Opt for the usual furniture:

- A table, a chair, a bookcase and a shelf for toys – pay attention to the Drommel x Superludi collaboration. This is a fantastic example of simple concise solutions that are suitable for any interior;
- Or give rein to your imagination. For example, cut down the legs of a regular table so that it's comfortable and suitable for the child's height;
- A wardrobe + portable footrest. The latter one is sold at IKEA and will be useful throughout the apartment where a small child lives;
- A standard size bed;
- An ordinary, "non-baby" carpet.

Explorer's room checklist:

☐ wardrobe
☐ table and a chair
☐ bed
☐ footrest
☐ bookshelves and books by age
☐ rug
☐ bed linen of neutral tones – 2 pcs

- [ ] set: a pillow + 2 types of blankets – for winter and summer
- [ ] bedspread: it should be so light that the child can make the bed on its own
- [ ] some funny bright interior cushions
- [ ] family photo
- [ ] picture or a poster (excluding anything that is childish)
- [ ] schedule / planning board
- [ ] some plants
- [ ] nightlight
- [ ] humidifier
- [ ] some aroma diffusers or a Berger lamp
- [ ] nest of shelves or chest of drawers for toys
- [ ] vase for fresh flowers

I want to draw attention to the last point in particular. Flowers are just as important for children as they are for adults. For boys and girls alike. The boys understand that this is a part of people's lives, wordless contact and attention, and a room with flowers becomes more cozy. Tell them what flowers you like and how beautiful they are. Thus, you cultivate a fine taste and emphasize the importance of the little things. On the contrary, you should give flowers to girls – even the smallest ones are able to put them in a vase. These girls grow up kind and loving. The children will do everything themselves or ask you for your advice. You are the best example, because in your room everything is exactly the way you like! Once in your room, the children find themselves in the world of their mother, and this causes a desire to create their own one:

"Mummy, where does this abacus come from?"
"And where did you get this green decanter?"
"Why are there cacti everywhere, Muuum?"
"I love this soft pillow so much!"
"Muuum, you smell so delicious!"
"Can I play here for a minute?"

Leave the children alone and live your life.

Individuality – 11 and older

There are really only two ways of decorating a teen's room:

You either tie them up, or negotiate with them.

We choose the second way and the first thing to remember (in fact, this is the basic principle of decorating a teen's room) is a **compromise**.

A teenager's room is, first of all, your lifeline and an opportunity to share the ever changing interests of a child, to get closer to him or her.

Our children can stay in their room for days on end, because for them it is the whole world.

First of all, talk to them, consider some ideas. Remember an important rule of this conversation – no imposed decisions. The main director is your child, and they grow up in the process of making their own decisions. Let them be aware of those aspects of their personality that may be revealed in the process of organizing space. Give your child an opportunity to express, create and be themselves. I suggest you and your child create a shared folder on Pinterest, and gather all of their ideas there.

There is no point in investing in paintings, because a teens' interests change very quickly, and there is nothing easier than just changing another poster.

The coolest **life hack** I can advise to a teenager's parents is a large table with more than one, and preferably with two or three workspaces: one for creativity, another one for homework and study.

Today's children are extremely overwhelmed, and two workspaces will help save time. For example, when he or she is doing homework, they can quickly switch, move to another workspace, and finish their drawing.

Fresh flowers also have a place in a teen's room. Firstly, it develops a sense of taste and beauty. Secondly, it is an extra reminder that you care about them.

Sometimes we don't have time to follow the new hobbies of our child, but don't rush to put all of their musical instruments away, even if they no longer play them. Such things shape a person, even if they are not being used.

Let your teen's interests and hobbies find a reflection in the decoration of their room: whether it's a stretching swing or a collection of basketballs.

Modern teenagers have a lot to keep in mind, so it's great when their plans and schedule are in front of their eyes. You can use mood boards for this.

Involve your teenagers in the implementation of their ideas, so that they love their space even more and show their creativity.

Checklist for a teen's room (but here it is important that he or she chooses things to their liking):

- ☐ bed
- ☐ set of pillows and blankets for 2 seasons
- ☐ bed linen – 2 sets
- ☐ bedspread
- ☐ bedside table or a cabinet
- ☐ large table with two workspaces
- ☐ shelf for textbooks
- ☐ table lamp
- ☐ computer or a laptop
- ☐ light (a floor lamp, a night light or battery-powered flashlights)
- ☐ plants and a watering can;
- ☐ flower vase
- ☐ backpack hook
- ☐ mirror
- ☐ wardrobe
- ☐ some posters
- ☐ family photos
- ☐ mood board (find a perfect one in Drommel)
- ☐ musical instrument (at least ukulele or a flute)
- ☐ carpet
- ☐ water carafe and a glass
- ☐ 2 or 3 trays
- ☐ portable speaker
- ☐ sculpture and decorations
- ☐ something that reflects a child's hobby

Bedroom: the core of the house. Erotica and nothing more

Let me remind you of the bedroom functions:

- a good sleep
- filling
- sex and energy exchange
- rest
- self-development

Let's start with what absolutely shouldn't be in the bedroom:

✗ TV

The bedroom is the main core of your life. This is the abode of sleep, love, sex, energizing, and rest – so, there is no place for TV here.

✗ **Unnecessary things:** things that clutter up, crowd the space – and most importantly, take away your energy.

Checklist of necessary things for the bedroom:

☐ **A glass and a carafe**

To drink a glass of water after waking up is a good habit. For that, you will need a carafe with water and some glasses. And let them be at hand, not in the kitchen, but right in the bedroom.

☐ **A small dish**

For pills, vitamins that you need to take in the morning, or different little things like rings and earrings.

☐ **Bed linen**

Choosing bed linen is a very personal and even intimate task. Some are delighted with the coolness and smoothness of silk, others prefer soft flannel and still others the naturalness of linen, someone is delighted with the dense and airy washed cotton, and someone is happy with smooth satin or textured percale. For myself, I chose bed linen on 📷 laurel_home made of soft French linen – the leader of trends for many decades.

Linen is a traditional material for bedding. Linen bedding is the most wear-resistant, which means it will last a long time and you do not have to spend a lot of time for taking care of it. Therefore, such bed linen is a profitable and long-lasting purchase.

The great advantage of linen is the fact that this fabric perfectly absorbs moisture, creating conditions for comfortable sleep. In summer, it creates a pleasant feeling of a slightly cool surface of the bed.

For the guests, I chose luxurious and high-quality bed linen of Italian production La Perla Home.

There should be only 2 sets of bed linen, and it would be nice if one of them was white.

The choice is yours, but if two people sleep in a bed, you should have four pillows and four blankets.

☐ **Blankets**

One option is lighter, the second is warmer. In addition, the multi-layer blankets will create an incredible coziness.

☐ **Bedspread**

You should not have it sewn from the same fabric as the curtains, plus you should buy it in specialized stores. You need to purchase a light bedspread that covers only a third of the bed. How to make the bed properly can be found here:

☐ **Plaid to wrap up if you suddenly want to lie down on the bedspread**

Plaid has long ceased to be just a functional element of decoration. Pinterest is full of pictures where plaid is the center of the composition or "killer feature" of the bedroom. For me, this is the main symbol of comfort. It definitely shouldn't be "boring", it should be something original, "extraordinary".

For example, in Woolkrafts plaids there is always something unusual: a combination of colors, interesting patterns and unique images. For example, a plaid with a map of Kiev, a plaid-cactus or a plaid Porto with a landscape of the coast in Portugal.

☐ **Painting, poster**

I recommend everyone to invest in at least one painting by a famous artist. Posters can be hung on the wall or placed on a chest of drawers. The bedroom is exactly the place where there should be a lot of art! Paintings of erotic content are worth buying, but this does not mean

that they should depict naked bodies. Rather, it is your inner beautiful erotic association. Pay attention to the paintings of Egon Schiele, René Magritte, Georgia O'Keefe, the Pirelli calendar 2014 by Helmut Newton, and of course do not forget about the photos of Robert Mapplthorpe, posters from the series "The Young Pope", illustrations by Leonor Fini, Dali "The Great Masturbator", Gustav Courbet "The Origin of the World" – this is only a small part of the works which I got to know from the participants of the #watchtowant marathon of visual experience, which I organized a year ago.

- ☐ **Book**

In the bedroom, leave only those books that you are actually reading now. Take books you don't read to the bathroom as a reminder to read them. Books that you have already read – in the living room, as a reminder that you are great and have already read them.

- ☐ **Music speaker**

It will allow you to connect and talk on speakerphone or listen to meditative music before going to bed.

- ☐ **Big flowerpot**, even huge!

It should be big, even for a small bedroom it is air. One may be enough.

- ☐ **Two vases**

In one there is always a pot that can be changed, for example, bonsai, moss. Anything, but it should be in a vase. The second is a vase that will invite your loved one to give you flowers… or tell you to buy them for yourself. They have to be side by side. Instead of a tray under the vases, you can use a mirror.

- ☐ **Photos**

You can put your photos, family photos, photos of dogs and other pets on the chest of drawers near the posters – they evoke gratitude and a sense of happiness.

- ☐ **Rugs**

Put rugs where you step barefooted when you get out of bed and in front of the bed. When we get out of bed, we want to step on a pleasant tactile covering. We use them in front of the bed, to create a general integral image.

- **Bedside cabinet** (the next chapter is devoted to it)
- **Aroma candles**, humidifiers, aroma lamps
- **Ladder.** It is an ideal item of decor and storage of bedspreads and blankets, as well as a bathrobe.
- **Minimum 4 light sources.** Think of lighting, of bedside light, of half-light.
- **Curtains** that do not let in light. To do this, you can use a roll blackout on the window, and add coziness with the linen curtains.

Do not forget about personification. When entering your bedroom, you have to feel that you live here, not a stranger.

Bedside cabinets – 27 variations, no classic styles

The functions of our bedside cabinet:

- convenience;
- turning routines into rituals (morning glass of water, meditation, and so on);
- aesthetic pleasure.

Bedside cabinet is an extremely convenient thing, because you always have at hand what you may need in the evening, at night or in the morning: book / glass of water / charger and nightlight.

> **Important!** Put a vase with fresh flowers or a floor standing flowerpot next to it. The plant will combine the bed and bedside cabinet into a single ensemble, and the vase will remind you that the bedroom is the place where you care about yourself.

You can place a small dish for jewelry and a mini music speaker on the bedside cabinet.

In general, an irreplaceable thing!

Well, remember what we've learned in the previous chapter about eclecticism: at least a third of your interior should be art objects. Recently, I discovered such bedside tables – art objects of Ukrainian production 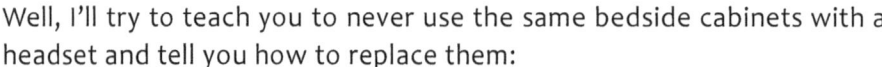 decor2art, and was pleasantly surprised by their unusual shapes, bold combinations and colors. The day I posted them on Instagram and was bombarded with questions about them, I realized that you, my readers, also like this art form. It seems to me that the girls were not ready for such a stir then, but now they have adapted to it and regularly please themselves with new things.

Well, I'll try to teach you to never use the same bedside cabinets with a headset and tell you how to replace them:

- vintage chair with a high back and a wooden seat. A very good solution! You can hang a dressing gown or a bedspread on it
- bar table
- floating shelf by the bed with a pinch lamp
- ladder
- old chest

- iron stool + wooden tray underneath
- hanging swing
- block system behind the bed
- lamp + iron hinged box
- chest of drawers of small height
- round clay table
- acrylic toilet table
- wooden old stool or stool of fancy shape
- high-tech (iron cube)
- shelf for flowerpots
- coffee table
- stack of books or magazines
- old drum
- chair with straw back thonet
- glowing acrylic cube
- console
- ceramic Chinese chair
- wooden log
- wooden or iron barrel
- iron storage basket
- other objects that have horizontal flat area and a little higher than a bed.

I recommend to store on all these surfaces:

- ☐ carafe of water and a glass
- ☐ vase
- ☐ flowerpot
- ☐ lamp
- ☐ small dish for little things
- ☐ aroma candle

Bathroom – the skin of your home

What is a bathroom?

This place is deliberate. Even, I would say, sacred.

It performs several functions:

- cleanses your body
- disciplines you to take care of yourself and devote time to yourself
- serves as a tool for self-awareness
- gives time to be alone with your thoughts
- sets you for the day
- relaxes at night
- inspires
- gives an opportunity to relax

The main mistake that many people make is that the bedroom should be much more beautiful than the bathroom. But no, no! Stop it! Arrange beautiful storage racks, hang pictures! They will not be cheap, but they will give you joy forever and a day.

I adore #bathroomasaspa, because that is the exact philosophy of this space.

Bathroom checklist:

- ☐ paintings / posters / photos
- ☐ speaker
- ☐ towels of the same color
- ☐ soap and hand cream
- ☐ soft mats
- ☐ greenery
- ☐ toilet paper basket
- ☐ chair or a stool
- ☐ candles and aroma candles
- ☐ ladder
- ☐ storage systems
- ☐ diffuser / perfume for the bathroom
- ☐ clock
- ☐ ring stand / jewelry plate
- ☐ art object
- ☐ bathtub book holder
- ☐ mirrors
- ☐ books and magazines
- ☐ hourglass
- ☐ bathrobe

Homework:

1. Collect and save bathroom inspiration on Pinterest, shifting the focus from tiles and plumbing to decorative things: posters, greenery, other décor from our checklist, make yourself a "spabouquet". How to make it?

2. Make a bouquet of spicy herbs and branches (verbena, eucalyptus, rosemary and mint) and hang it on the shower watering can so that there is no direct interaction between herbs and water. The hot steam will release essential oils and fill the bath with the aroma of the spa.

Kitchen affairs

"In my opinion, people are naturally divided into guests and hosts."
© *Vogue*

We know that the most important issues are resolved there.

"Think like a store owner," says the chapter of the book Remodelista by J. Carlson and M. Guralnik. Well, applying the rules of merchandising in your kitchen is not such a bad idea!

All the retailers are fighting for eye-level space, so place items that you use often in your line of sight and those that you use less often either higher or lower. In general, you do not need shelves on which you can place more than two rows of things – you just will not see them there.

The only rule of merchandising which is not suitable for us: no empty shelves. I am convinced that an empty shelf in the kitchen is our basic need (and not only in the kitchen). That is why I dedicated a separate chapter to this topic.

When organizing a kitchen, we start with its functions.

The kitchen is one of the most visited places in the house.

If you do not consider it as a utility room, then it has many functions: from the workplace to the gathering place of the whole family.

I consider you and myself exclusively as homemakers, so I repeat the six main functions of the kitchen:

- cooking
- storing utensils and appliances
- storing food
- eating
- communication
- work

For you, the kitchen is a full-fledged office, and it should be approached as a workplace if you are:

- a home confectioner
- engaged in producing frozen semi-finished products or home canning
- a professional space organizer
- a food photographer
- a food blogger
- a food stylist

And if it is necessary with no delay:

- to expose light
- to buy a huge refrigerator (for the confectioner)
- to create beautiful background when recording the recipe
- to equip cupboards with props

I usually see 5 "problem" places in almost every kitchen:

1. Too many useless things (they make kitchens look untidy and demotivate us to spend time there);
2. There are almost no storage systems;
3. Acute lack of beautiful non-kitchen items (lamps, books, candles, vases and flowerpots);
4. Ill-considered space around the dining table (and this is very important!);
5. Lack of visible signs of rituals and trays with objects used for them.

I suggest walking through all the "problem" places, starting with the last one:

5. LACK OF VISIBLE SIGNS OF RITUALS AND TRAYS WITH OBJECTS USED FOR THEM

They should be seen with the naked eye. Create kitchen areas for your rituals: for coffee, food, etc. Collect the necessary items on trays: this is how the kitchen looks neat.

Such rituals could be, and on such trays you could place, the following:

- candle, glass of wine (water) during dinner
- tea / coffee corner
- ritual of self-care (decanter, water, dietary supplements or vitamins)
- other visual images of rituals

4. ILL-CONSIDERED SPACE AROUND DINING TABLE

If the dining table is in the kitchen, then there should be a chest of drawers next to it, which will store:

- tablecloths and napkins, candles and everything for serving
- beautiful sets and utensils
- cutlery
- tea and coffee sets

3. ACUTE LACK OF BEAUTIFUL NON-KITCHEN ITEMS

Add something old. In general, everything new is fantastically transformed in the presence of the old – it is the law. Pay attention to materials, warm colors are the priority. Say "Yes" to unexpected combinations! Where else, if not in the kitchen, can you experiment? Avoid unnatural colors. Don't buy things that are too bright (unless it's a SMEG kettle from the D&G collection).

Crystal – yes!

Clay – yes!

Sculptures and candles that "kill" the smells of cooking – yes. (Unless it's the smell of fresh croissants).

What things can be considered as non-kitchen items:

- paintings and posters
- candlesticks and candles
- vases
- books, except culinary
- vases
- mirrors
- sculptures
- third light

2. ALMOST NO STORAGE SYSTEMS

The inside should be more beautiful than the outside! Buy cute and convenient storage containers. They are not cheap, but they will serve and bring you joy for a long time.

If you compare a dress that you wear only once, with a dress that you wear 100 times, then at the same price the latter will actually be a gift to you.

Draw a scenario of cooking, for example, pasta: get the pasta, then salt, spices, sauce…etc. Think about storage so that getting it all was convenient.

> **Important!** Perfectly organized storage is achieved when a stranger can easily cook scrambled eggs in your home! Follow the French rule mise en place, which literally means EVERYTHING IS IN ITS PLACE.

I like to store plates and appliances in a drawer at the bottom: it is convenient to put a distributor for plates with adjustable size range and apertures for appliances.

Store food properly in separate cabinets and special containers, without mixing with utensils and kitchen appliances.

It will be ideal if you can allocate separate cabinets for:

- bulk products: pasta, cereals, flour, sugar and salt
- oils and liquids
- canning: beans, peas, corn (that which is not necessary to store in the refrigerator)
- tea, coffee, sweets
- vegetables that cannot be stored in the refrigerator

Tip: allocate a separate box for towels next to the sink at arm's length.

1. TOO MANY USELESS THINGS

The list of basic things will be discussed in the next section.

Ask yourself:

"What do I use all the time?" It is very important to focus on these things and get rid of stuff you don't use.

There should be neither more nor less than the "lagom", as the Swedes say. We become hostages of things by serving them. Personally, I am not ready to serve them.

Kitchen utensils: quantity and other secrets

All kitchen utensils are divided into seven categories:

1. preparation
2. cooking
3. baking
4. serving
5. storing food
6. appliances
7. other

I once studied at the School of Restaurateurs in Kyiv-Mohyla Business School and got many great pieces of advice there. And although my experience in the restaurant business did not last long, I took some valuable habits with me.

Now I am happy to share them:

- buy in restaurant equipment stores. There I buy trays, pans, stainless steel pans and cutting boards;

- take an inventory of the kitchen at least once every two months – you will be surprised at how much junk accumulates there;

- first in, first out – this is the rule of storing food in the refrigerator all restaurateurs know. No less important is to check all expiration dates at least once a month.

Let's go through each of the items:

1. FOR PREPARATION OF INGRIDIENTS:

Basic list of necessary items, regardless of whether you live alone or with your family:

- 4 knives: bread, multi-chef, small (for convenience) and for slicing vegetables
- 4 cutting boards (do not be afraid to buy wooden)
- vegetable peeler
- grater
- kitchen scissors
- bottle opener
- colander

- whisk
- tweezers (to get bones from fish)

2. FOR COOKING: You will need

- 4 pans: 3-liter casserole with lid, 5-6-liter casserole with lid for pasta, 2 saucepans
- 2 cast iron pans (20-25 cm and 16-18 cm)
- cauldron
- wood spoon
- spatula
- meat thermometer

3. FOR BAKING:

- two sets of measuring cups (one for liquids, the other for bulk)
- scales
- three containers of different sizes for mixing (ideal Joseph&Joseph, which is sold with measuring spoons and is easy to store)
- shallow baking tray
- two baking tins
- cake pan with lid

4. FOR SERVING:

For a family of four it is enough to have:

- 6 cups for tea
- 6 cups for coffee (I adore with a double bottom)
- 6 plates with a diameter of 21-23 cm
- 6 multi-functional glasses made of thick glass (suitable for juice, coffee, tea, spirits, liqueurs, water)
- 6 dessert plates
- 6 bowls (for salads and soups)
- 6 pieces of cutlery (fork, knife, spoon and small pastry fork, teaspoon)
- 2 wineglasses
- 2 decanters of different sizes
- 2 large dishes

- thermos teapot for serving and soulful evenings
- bread box for storage and serving
- 4-5 salad bowls of different diameters
- 2-3 tablecloths (both white and colored)
- 2-3 sets of placemats
- 2-3 vases
- 1-2 trays

5. FOR STORING FOOD:

- for storing food in the fridge
- for storing spices, cereals, etc. in the kitchen.

The next chapter is about the fridge and its contents are waiting for us.

To store spices and cereals we will need:

- a set of quality glass containers for storing cereals
- containers for storing spices – I use 📷 noeledwood
- tin cans
- waxed napkins
- cloth bags for groceries
- clips for them
- stickers and markers
- paper bags
- trays for grouping spices and cereals on shelves

6. KITCHEN APPLIANCES:

- tea maker
- toaster
- oven
- fridge
- mortar for spices
- blender or food processor
- coffee maker
- kettle
- mixer

7. OTHER:

- gloves
- 4 kitchen towels
- 4-6 trays
- a trivet

The rest can be, if it is:

- very good, and you cannot live without it;
- performs the necessary functions personally for you.

Almost all the items from our seven categories of kitchen utensils can be found in brick and mortar shops or on the website of POSUDMEISTER.

There is everything there: from bone china to handmade copper utensils from the Italian masters of the house Ruffoni! Pay special attention to copper pots and pans, they will add comfort to almost any kitchen.

Suddenly, we will have an empty shelf in the kitchen. I'll talk about it in a separate section, but believe me, it's worth living in your home.

Fridge and its contents

Why should we worry about the fridge?

The main rule of a cozy house: inside should be more beautiful than outside.

The fridge belongs to the touchpoints, i.e. to the list of things we touch more than 4 times a day, and its interior should bring us joy. It is very important!

An American, Rob Greenfield (@ robjgreenfield), photographs food from garbage cans to show how much we throw away.

With a properly organized fridge, we will not throw away food (according to statistics, 20% of everything purchased in stores, we throw away).

That is, the money spent on the purchase of utensils, we will return within the next few months, without buying extra.

As a starter kit we will need:

- ☐ 12-16 glass food storage containers with lids (of different sizes)
- ☐ Stickers for labels
- ☐ 1 marker
- ☐ 3 cups of rigid plastic for greens
- ☐ 2-3 wicker iron baskets
- ☐ 2-3 glass jars with lids of 0.7-1 l
- ☐ 2-3 jars with lids of 0.4-0.5 liters
- ☐ 2 odor absorbers
- ☐ 5-6 waxed napkins
- ☐ 3-4 enameled containers for marinating fish and meat.

Separately I want to tell you about waxed napkins. Incredible luxury and 100% sustainability! What it is? Wax or waxed napkins are reusable wrappers that are used to store food instead of cling film.

The main thing you need to know is that they are 100 percent safe and incredibly beautiful. Ingredients: cotton, beeswax, jojoba oil, cold-pressed coconut oil, highest grade wood resins. Everything I do is always about benefits, but also about the aesthetics of everyday life. About the education of taste and every day beauty. It is important for me to take care of the planet and the health of my loved ones, but it is important to do it in an aesthetic way. I'm talking about balance in everything.

You can buy it all here:

- www.ikea.com
- www.granit.com
- www.AliExpress.com

Homework:

Clean the whole fridge at least once a month; arrange a separate shelf for:

- dairy products
- meat and fish (below, exclusively)
- greens, fruits and vegetables that can be stored in the fridge
- ready meals or its ingredients

One empty shelf

According to my method of arranging the house, the basic need is to have at least one completely empty shelf: in the closet, in the kitchen, among other places of storage.

It is very functional:

- If one of the guests brings gifts, we put them there without disturbing the decoration of the room and festive moment;
- Bringing home stuff that I have not found a place for yet. It is a "temporary" place of living;
- This shelf serves as a temporary depot when you move something from the crammed shelves (for example, glasses from the back row);
- It serves as a reminder of things that need to be repaired. Yes, when you put a wooden board there, you will remember that it needs to be greased with oil. In fact, the board can be there until the oil is completely absorbed.

As you can see, such an unpretentious thing as a free shelf will significantly help maintain order not only in the kitchen, but also "in your head".

An empty shelf has a very positive effect on the emotional state of the person – it shows a state of calmness.

Even if you have a very small closet – find a place for one empty shelf.

Dining table at which no one sits

There is no sight duller than a dining table at which no one sits. Although it can also become the epicenter of comfort in the kitchen and dining room!

A vase with flowers (if you are lucky!) or a vase for fruit are all you should place on it.

I suggest making this still life more diverse.

To do this, you will need a simple formula

$$A\ table = A + B + C$$

A. Mirror
A. Wooden board
A. Tray
A. Tablecloth, napkin or runner

B. Hourglass
B. Three or four candles of various levels and shapes with candlesticks
B. A vase with flowers or with branches (in winter)
B. Multi-layer tray (for nuts and dried fruits)
B. Several vases for a flower
B. A book and the flowerpot on it
B. A sculpture
B. Battery-powered electric candle
B. Battery-powered garland
B. Fruit vase

C. Carafe with water and glasses
C. "Tactile item" is something that is pleasant to touch: stone, bronze, porcelain, felt. Any little thing that is nice to take in your hands.

Homework:

1. Make at least six combinations with the formula from this section.
2. Think about where you can take these items.

A basic set for holidays and table setting exists!

Arranging beautiful meals and being able to do it blindfolded is your main task. If you still don't do so now, you can easily choose serving options on the Internet.

The task of this section is to understand how and why to serve a table for every meal and what to buy for decoration for all occasions and holidays.

The table should always be set.

Let it be a basic table setting (see Lazy Serving below), but it's a must-have.

If you have some inspiration – organize a holiday or themed setting.

Alternatively, if your family has a holiday, then the responsibility for its beauty lies on your shoulders. You can order prepared meals, but you have to make it look like a holiday and add some energy and soulfulness to it.

Thus, the table setting consists of:

- serving breakfast / lunch / dinner
- serving food

In turn, serving breakfast / lunch / dinner, is divided into several types:

- leisurely / weekend serving
- serving for the lazy
- bed serving
- holiday / themed serving

Furthermore, **serving breakfast**, which is the most important meal and sets the mood for the whole day. Everyone likes taking pictures of beautiful breakfasts, not even mentioning the fact that everyone likes eating a nice breakfast! However, I am surprised that not many people prepare and serve them at all, though it is a colossal energy exchange.

Lunch Serving. It may sound strange, but I advise you not to have lunch at home. Keith Ferrazzi in his Never Eat Alone book suggests developing the habit of dining in a cafe. You can't disagree with his idea, because it is a great opportunity to decorate your life with interesting interlocutors.

Dinner Serving. We use standard lazy serving + add candles. That's the whole secret.

Serving for the lazy consists of:

- an original cup
- a placemat
- a single flower vase
- a small plate at the top right corner for details (some bread, jam, butter, chocolate)

- plates
- cutlery

Leisurely / weekend serving:

- arrange large plates (diameter 23-25 cm)
- put pre-folded into a rectangle napkins on them
- put smaller plates on top
- place cutlery to the right and left of each plate: a fork on the left, a knife on the right
- put glasses for water and drinks
- add a decanter
- place a flower arrangement

If you have inspiration, use a certain amount of decorations from the "For All Occasions" list.

Bed Serving:

For this serving you need the largest tray from the "For All Occasions" list, a single flower vase, a drink (coffee, tea, Prosecco) and one small heart shaped plate, or one with a funny face on it (you can find them in ceramic shops). Don't overload the tray – you're not really going to eat.

Holiday / Themed Serving:

This serving is necessary when there is a holiday in the house. Without inspiration or with it, but use EVERYTHING from the "For All Occasions" list. You may ask where to put the food then, as the whole table is occupied by decorations. Here the Swedes come to the rescue with their invention – a buffet. You set all the food on a separate small side table or on the kitchen counter, the guests put the food on their plates and return to their beautiful table.

There are only 4 secrets of the buffet.

They are the basic serving of dishes:

- crumpled parchment (tear some pieces off parchment, crumple them, and then unfold and put them under the dishes!)
- greens (grow them in a pot on the windowsill)
- multilevel

- a bright accent in the middle (a vase with some branches, flowers, a sculpture – anything).

You should take care of the base for all holidays:

New Year, Christmas, Easter, Mother's Day, Father's Day, Kupala Night, birthdays, professional holidays.

All the holidays will be fun and successful, if you only change the entourage.

For example, you put some lemons in a round wide low glass vase in summer, in winter – you put some cones, at Kupala Night – you float candles on the water.

Now finally "For All Occasions", the **checklist for serving and decoration:**

- ☐ an iron ice bucket (it can be used not only for ice and bottles, but also for flowers)
- ☐ two tablecloths (white and colored), a table runner, placemats, cloth napkins. I often use and am partial to 📷 nest.homegoods – they are linen, with a huge selection of interesting colors and size.

> **Important!** Napkins can be simply tied in a knot and placed on or under a plate.

- ☐ 2-3 trays of different diameters to choose from:
   – wooden tray with sides
   – iron oval one
   – porcelain round tray with lid
- ☐ marble or stone heavy tray
- ☐ mirror tray
- ☐ rose bowl
- ☐ flat horizontal low sculpture
- ☐ sectioned bowl with 4-5 compartments; a wide scented candle in glass or ceramics
- ☐ multilevel tray
- ☐ 2-3 black iron baskets
- ☐ 3-4 wooden chopping boards
- ☐ 6 candles of the same color
- ☐ some tea lights

- ☐ modern candlesticks of different height
- ☐ narrow neck single flower vase
- ☐ vintage bronze / brass candlestick
- ☐ ordinary business cards without inscriptions (yes, you simply order plain white business cards)
- ☐ placemats (plate holders)
- ☐ thick glasses. At home, you can drink from any tableware you want, and it doesn't have to be a classic cup with a handle. For coffee and tea, for example, use thick glass cups, in contrast, you can use a thin glass teapot instead. You can also complement the glasses made of thick glass with the thin glasses, because there is usually more than one drink, so you can pour yourself some juice and some water
- ☐ water decanter
- ☐ a nice set
- ☐ small heart or fish shaped plates

Rules:

1. Play with textures: iron + wood + glass + porcelain + clay + flowers;
2. Combine all the materials on one tablecloth, grouping them on a tray;
3. Place accents (sign the prepared cards with cute inscriptions).

What shall I do?

Gather it all on one shelf and never again spend time thinking about how to set a table.

Creative table decoration and broken dishes

Let's talk about lonely plates, cups and other tableware.

What to do with broken plates?

In fact, they can be used for:

- serving meals
- solo serving (for example, a selfish breakfast)
- table setting

You need to make room for all kinds of serving, making each one of them count, provided that the following 2 rules are followed:

1. The item is unique and you like it (if you like it, it is already unique), but isn't just some random assortment. As my subscriber ⓘ annadarial wrote in a comment to a post about out of sync serving: "I, as a coherent serving expert, can't imagine a black luminarc plate and a worn-out set, given to somebody 16 years ago for their wedding by their classmates, together on anyone's table!" You totally don't need things that do not bring you joy in your apartment, even if they are plates that serve as a food stand. After all, the function is only the first note of our song.

2. The item is made of noble or interesting materials: iron, silver, brass, copper, plastic, glass, crystal, etc.

Step 1. Put these items together.

Think about the best way to combine them. Just as decorators combine different paintings with a single color on the wall or the same picture frames, or furniture from different eras with a carpet.

Similarly, cracked dishes should be combined with one element and a leitmotif, so that it's not a frog quartet, but a well-coordinated brass band.

This unifying "something" could be:

- a tablecloth
- cutlery
- placemats
- runners
- napkins and textiles
- basic set of plates

Step 2: buy 6 basic plates of the same color.

Tip: it is good to mix the random dishes with the basic sets of dishes.

Option 1: replace one or two plates with vintage, bright or themed ones.

Step 3. Go to your wardrobe.

It is very important to use something interesting in addition to single plates to maintain the rhythm of the table.

- Option 1: use rings and jewelry instead of napkin rings
- Option 2: use glasses of different heights, shapes and colors
- Option 3: use different vintage non-kitchen items (sculptures, flower arrangements) and candles with different candlesticks.

 Interesting!

There is a great rule for beautiful table setting: all plates should be different.

Well-known brands, including Fornasetti, Ibride, Villeroy & Boch and others, have sets of dishes with different prints, but of the same size.

My favorite Seletti use the Japanese kintsugi technique – gluing together two plates of different shape and style. So if you set different plates for guests, it will look very beautiful, believe me. This is provided that the two conditions I've mentioned above are met.

A piece of advice from me:

if you follow the "theme" and buy, for example, items of the same color or geometry from different manufacturers – you will get an incredible setting. For example, buy black and white checkered or graphic design plates from different manufacturers – from new to vintage, and you will gradually collect your unique service! It takes long time, but it's worth it.

Tip number infinity:

Buying in pairs is perfect! In this way you increase the rhythm of the table, this technique especially helps to duplicate the serving at both ends of the table (which is incredibly convenient and helps to avoid large structures in the center).

What to do with broken dishes from the English collection? How to throw away the finest Chinese porcelain of incredible blue color or say goodbye to a beautiful set that reminds you of childhood and the smell of tangerines?

Broken tableware / pottery is one of the world's greatest inspirations.

Antoni Gaudi and his friend Josep Jujol went to the dumpsters of ceramic workshops, tile factories and glass-blowing enterprises and made their entire works of art, known as broken tile mosaics, out of fragments of the remains. This technique is called Trencadis, and it has seeped into the life of modernism from Barcelona. Many of you have seen souvenirs made of pieces of tile.

Ironically, Santiago Calatrava, a famous Spanish architect, also builds from pieces of tiles, but with a small remark: these tiles are specially made for him.

I am also madly in love with the kintsugi technique, a Japanese art of restoring ceramics using lacquer made from the sap of lacquer trees mixed with gold, silver or platinum powder. The philosophical basis of the art of kintsugi is, first of all, that cracks are inseparable from the history of an object and therefore do not deserve to be forgotten and disguised. For God's sake! That is the most romantic thing I've ever heard!

> **Tip:** I strongly recommend collecting beautiful broken dishes in a lovely box and read the chapter of this book about hobbies and a place for solitude. It seems to be a very inspiring activity. I have already bought everything I need for kintsugi.

Homework:

1. Collect several options of creative serving.
2. Make a list of items in your house that can become the pearls of this serving and make a list of desired items.

Reception and guest room

I would like to express my gratitude to Catherine and Gleb Zagoria, whose reception inspired me to write this chapter.

Friends are a family we choose!

Who has never had any guests? In this chapter, I'm going to talk about my approach to receiving guests and the secrets that help me enjoy it.

As for me, the most important thing is their experience, the experience they have at my place.

You can divide the text (and the chapter) into two parts: short time receptions with meals and overnight guest receptions.

These two experiences differ from each other both in rhythm and tactics.

Let's take a look at both options and their differences.

IF THE GUESTS STAY OVERNIGHT, YOUR HOUSE TURNS INTO A HOTEL

It is your responsibility to provide the following set, per guest, in the guest room (if there isn't one, just keep this set for guests in your closet):

- 2 towels (a bath and hand towel)
- toothbrush
- toothpaste
- bathrobe
- set of entertaining magazines or a new book
- set of bed linen
- compliment (e.g. a postcard saying "What happens in this house stays in this house", a pack of chewing gum and condoms).

I love gaining experience in different hotels and implementing it in the home, whilst receiving guests. The first (and the most important) thing in hotels is a good mattress and bed linen.

I feel like a true fairy when I hear the feedback of my guests about unforgettable nights spent as if they were sleeping on a soft and light cloud. To achieve this, I used the principle, "Always give a little more than you can afford" and bought quality textiles from La Perla Home Macrame for the guest bedroom.

In premium hotels, I've seen schedules where the main entertainment events are listed for the period of stay. Why not to learn from this wonderful experience? You can make the following schedule:

wake up time (this will help "unload" the bathroom and avoid crowding), personal time and meal times.

If you have a separate room, it's great. In fact, this is a hotel room in your home. However, if you don't have a separate room, you can use something else: a kid's room, your bedroom, a part of the living room (but it temporarily ceases to be "common"). Giving more than you can is your main principle of receiving guests, which brings you a lot of joy and energy.

COOKING AND EATING

Be sure to involve guests in your routine. You can cook together, set the table together and clean up together. It is good to have some interactivity during the meal like fondue or mini-grill. It's perfect for the rhythm of breakfast / lunch / dinner.

For entertainment you can play some board games: Dixit, Memology, Charades, Rummikub.

It's a good idea to prepare for a photo shoot together and do it.

It's also good to make something together:

- paint a picture
- make a collage
- repaint old furniture
- make a complex dessert
- start your own hashtag or rubric
- write a letter to yourself in 5 years

IF YOUR GUESTS ARE NOT GOING TO STAY OVERNIGHT, THE BEST ADVICE IS TO FOLLOW THE RHYTHM AND STICK TO IT

My secret to receiving guests for one evening (or lunch-dinner) is "changing locations". You must change three locations in the house.

THE FIRST LOCATION – APERITIF

A beautiful balcony or terrace would be perfect for this part.

We will need:

- large wooden chopping board
- parchment paper (you crumple and straighten it out)
- some snacks

- Prosecco / lemonade / cider
- wine glasses
- decanter with water (you may add some mint or lemon) and water glasses
- music

Don't make this mistake! When your guests arrive, don't invite them to the table and hastily try to finish cooking. If you do not have time, it's OK! I assure you, the guests don't just come to eat. Got it? As soon as the guests are on the doorstep, you smile, forget about everything and go for an aperitif.

Scientists say it takes at least 20 minutes to tune in to one another.

So we just sit, don't rush anywhere and tune in to one another with our guests for 20 minutes.

Mood: laughter, joy, news exchange.

THE SECOND LOCATION IS BREAKFAST / LUNCH / DINNER

After the aperitif, you can finish cooking your dinner. If you need help – ask for it.

It can be lunch at a table or an outdoor picnic.

To make everything beautiful and comfortable, we set 2 tables: one with food (a side table) and one beautifully set (see the "For All Occasions" section). Do not cook a lot of food; a main course and a side dish should be enough. Guests don't want to overeat either. Two dishes is best, but they should be interesting ones. New food experience – this is the leitmotif of our second location.

THE THIRD ONE – DIGESTIF

This should definitely be your third location.

The word digestif (borrowed from French) literally means, "that it aids digestion." This is the general name for drinks served after a meal.

The decorated and prepared in advance bar will allow you to finish the reception in a royal way, and while the guests are making their own drinks, you can change your clothes, bring small gifts for them or put the dishes in the dishwasher. First of all, you should make sure that there are enough different drinks to meet the tastes and needs of everyone.

Digestif is cognac, Armagnac or other types of brandy. This group also includes grappa, calvados, whiskey, liqueurs and balsams, as well as aged strong wines with rich flavors – Sherry, Madeira, and Port.

It isn't necessary to have a special place for this. It can be a vintage wheelbarrow table that can be easily moved around the house. One of the best suppliers of these tables is 🅘 Barhat.home.

By the way, the chair on the cover of this book is also from there!

The main secret of serving digestifs is a crystal decanter and small stemmed shot glasses. Even the most ordinary drinks in them will seem unusual to your guests. Just don't forget to sign the decanters, please.

Tip: trays will help maintain order and segment drinks and glasses so that they are easy to find. Plus, a book on brandy or wine will complement the digestif's atmosphere!

Put all unnecessary stuff away! As they say, less is more! However, don't forget about fruit (lemons and olives are perfect) and water, as they may serve as a snack and decor at the same time.

Mood: long conversations about everything in the world, summing up and plans.

Guest reception is by no means obligatory. I am sure that the skill of receiving guests is in your blood, and these secrets will allow you to enjoy the precious time spent together.

Workplace or home office

I want to share with you a funny fact about Truman Capote. The author of the all-time classic novel "Breakfast at Tiffany's" claimed to be a "horizontal writer" because he loved to write while lying in bed in the bedroom or on the couch in the living room with a cigarette and a cup of coffee. Coffee often slowly turned into mint tea, the tea into sherry, the sherry into martini… and this is how his immortal story "Breakfast at Tiffany's" was created.

I am talking about the fact that you don't need to organize the workplace just for the sake of its existence. Now, during this digital age, when a phone or a laptop is enough for work, you can do a great job by just moving around the house with your gadgets. But if you are not a "horizontal writer" and your effectiveness is decreasing, when there is no full-fledged workspace, it must be set up so that psychologically you can quickly switch to work.

The good news is that it doesn't necessarily has to be a separate office.

The good news is that it doesn't necessarily has to even be a desk.

The good news is that you can do it by yourself right now by placing an order for several components online.

And the best news is that it will not be me. It will be you. You are the person who organizes it for yourself.

So, where can your workplace be?

Firstly, it can be a kitchen: kitchen windowsill, part of the dining table, kitchen island.

Secondly, a living room / hall: table in front of a couch, coffee table, windowsills.

The bedroom is also an option: a wall unit, part of the closet (the part that will serve as a "map"), and it is attached to suitcases + chair, windowsills.

And in addition to the list: the corridor, balcony, easel.

MY GENERAL RECOMMENDATIONS AND IDEAS:

- free wall
- hanging shelf
- table lamp
- horizontal surface
- chair
- large mirror instead of a tabletop
- display in front of the table (there will be references attached to it and everything you will need for work)
- storages

Find unoccupied places in your home and fantasize about how they can be "reformatted". Remember what is important:

- convenience and order
- thoughtful additions
- flexibility
- "yes" to symmetry: paintings above the desktop, plants, books
- "no" to symmetry: not overdo it
- add "carelessness"
- cozy elements: posters, decanter, vase, flowers, candles, office organizers, portable speakers... things that add comfort and inspiration to you

SOLVING ORGANIZATIONAL ISSUES:

- if the table is old or flaky or you just don't like it – take the paints, a brush, painting tape and repaint it, change the handles. We make it an art object! Decoratorskyi paints and Barvaland are your reliable assistants!
- no space? Find a corner of 60 cm or add a new function to an existing piece of furniture
- no daylight or privacy? Use the elements, which are suitable. Don't forget about table lamps
- the unattractive back of the canvas – book covers, scrapbooking and paint will help!

TRANSFORMING MATERIALS THAT MAY BE USEFUL:

- shelf under the table
- canvas for any construction purpose: MDF, pressed MDF
- wooden board (you can make out of three + sandpaper grit 0)
- iron mood boards, corners, secretaire, corkboard, shelves for paintings, iron ropes for gallery wraps, net, organizers for vertical storage, reusable glue
- organizers – nets, felt – the more storage space a person has, the happier he is

GENERAL RULES OF THE WORKPLACE ORGANIZATION BY FUNCTIONS:

1. Creation of a "library" zone, where all the tasks (work, personal, development and leisure!) are done.

   So you can clearly see what baggage of knowledge you are going to carry with yourself. It also really helps to see the "obstacles". Do you remember that happiness comes from balance?

2. Creation of a workplace arranged for you – to which you gradually transfer tasks from the "library".

3. Sports corner with pre-loaded lessons. It's a single yoga mat for me!

4. Determining a place for the schedule, where you can see both general tasks without timing, as well as clearly planned tasks (skype calls / online classes, group classes).

5. Creating your own "star alley" with completed tasks / mind maps and goals (especially important for children).

Your workplace should be as comfortable as possible, give energy, inspire you. Just imagine – instead of a laptop on your couch – a cozy corner with water and decanter, stationery, lamp, speaker connected to the phone, clock, candle and humidifier.

I really like the slogan of the furniture company Drommel: "Home Office without excess: get rid of clutter, focus on the important things." This is manifest for those, who have accepted the challenge of energetic work and self-education at home instead of lounging on the couch.

Notes

Creative workshop is not a luxury

In any creative process, the ideal scenario is when "what" and "how" come at the same time. But it often happens like this: when we have inspiration, we don't have enough materials and time. When you bought the materials, the inspiration has run dry.

Therefore, in this section, we will make a list of basic creative things that will help you create when IT (Inspiration) has come.

I suggest you prepare and organize a minimum set in case of when inspiration "comes".

To this set, I would add:

- bird scissors (yes, those that even inspire in their form)
- glue gun
- liquid nails
- set of brushes and palette knives
- plasticine
- tablecloth (to cover the surface)
- gloves and apron
- several glass jars
- pencils
- acrylic paints
- pieces of fabric, ribbons, threads
- markers / felt tip pens
- thread and needle
- stationery knife
- set of paper
- watercolors
- notepad with a pen
- sketchbook
- masking tape

Remember that the organization is primary. All clear glass jars, iron boxes, and hanging organizers should be signed. If you have the perfect place – bingo! But to store these things, you can also use:

- portable table on wheels
- wardrobe
- corner on the balcony
- specially assembled box for creativity

I am almost sure that you already have an interesting hobby, but, if not, I recommend that you find it without wasting time. After all, having a hobby is just super important! Why? Because it's the best way to relieve stress and a great source of energy replenishment. Even at the end of the day, when it seems that you have neither moral nor physical strength left – doing what you love will make you much better than lying aimlessly on the couch and scrolling through social networks.

Because it makes you an even more interesting person and increases confidence and self-esteem. You will have new knowledge, experience, stories, and your circle of friends will grow. Because a person who is passionately and enthusiastically engaged in business looks extremely sexy in the eyes of his or her partner.

Because, as the saying goes, "An idle brain is a devil's workshop." A hobby will help you not only "switch off your brain" after work, but also turn it on when you start doing stupid things out of boredom.

Because it allows you to be yourself and reveal your inner child.

A true hobby is not a fashion trend; it is your pure pleasure without any obligations to society, family, or modern trends. This is the breath of fresh air, which gives a charge of bright emotions, relieves tension, and encourages personal growth.

Hobbies don't have to be the only ones for life, try different ones until you understand: "Yes, here it is!" and "How did I live without it all this time?" Do not look for external benefits when choosing a hobby – make a choice in line with your character. Hobbies have to be different, the variety of hobbies is important, but if you, like me, are a creative person, try the following options:

- sculpture
- painting
- growing indoor plants / ornamental trees
- wood carving
- modeling from clay, plasticine
- scrapbooking, quilling
- photos
- collecting
- collages
- floristry

When you decide on a choice, it is very important to buy and collect everything for this very hobby. Organize a kind of "Hobby Center" and create, create, create.

A place of solitude – a basic need

You really, really need a place to be alone, and here's why:
1. "Put your oxygen mask on first," before helping others – as the airplane instruction says. Obviously, you need to fill up somewhere, so taking care of such a place is just as important as fitting out a nursery, only even more important.
2. Loneliness and being alone are psychological needs of every person. Sooner or later, you will have an urgent need for this.
3. The ability to stop and check the "inner compass": am I going right, do I want to be there?

The higher a person's intelligence, the more time he or she needs to be alone. Such people live in a rich inner world, conduct dialogues with themselves, and ask themselves questions about crucial things for them.

I asked myself the question: What came first? The chicken or the egg? A place where you can be alone or the very desire for solitude? I think that if you did not have such a need – it will appear now, and it is worth fitting out such a place because it will improve the quality of your life. More efficiently = more consciously.

By analyzing each experience and drawing conclusions from it, you will make fewer mistakes.

For me, this is a super time of finding meaning, the very process of "thinking about a thought", savoring it, organizing plans, and a significant incentive for creativity. In private, I have incredible ideas, and I make significant discoveries. I really don't understand how people live without being able to be alone. After all, the growth of the soul is possible only in solitude, when no one is watching it.

Such a place can already exist. Don't look for difficult paths.

It can be in any room where:

1. There is a place to sit comfortably.
2. The rear is covered, and you feel safe.
3. There is cozy lighting.

A place of solitude is the third basic need (after flowers and an empty shelf).

You can sacrifice your interests for the sake of the common good, but it won't last long.

A place of solitude is exactly the place where you can entertain yourself without a phone: with a book, diary, candles, magazine, music speakers, plants, and the things you love.

Homework:

Write a list of activities for spending the time alone.

Living room is the brain of the house

Probably the greatest movement of our time, the importance of which is difficult to overestimate, is the struggle for gender equality, and as a result – neutral gender in the home.

Neutrality and tolerance are the motto of our time, and I really like it.

There are three doors in British public toilets: women's, men's and "sexless". No sex – no distortions.

In a gender-neutral home, all family members feel good and safe. So, there is an involvement in the general mood, but also the opportunity to stay in your comfort zone.

With such neutrality, both the brain and creativity work better. I would also like to mention the age asset: neutral and tolerant – so that it is optimal and comfortable for children, the elderly, young people and all age groups according to the WHO. This means you can say yes to anime posters, crochet baskets, a LEGO constructor, standing in the center of the living room, and cookbooks that can also stay right at the chess table.

Your direct task is to make everyone want to come to the living room and spend time there.

Engaging in different activities in one room is incredibly exciting. I imagine an English castle, where in the evenings all the family members gather in the fireplace hall and are going about their business. The father is citing Shakespeare's quotes, the mother is knitting, the daughter is practicing piano, the younger children are playing house, the sister's grandnephew is making a tower out of kitchen pots, and two grandparents (neighbours) are playing dominoes.

Without a TV, of course.

After all, the primary goal of the living room is communication and spending time together.

It's great to watch a movie together, but it is a pity that this is what almost every night of the average family is reduced to. However, now you know exactly what's the heart of the matter, and you understand that the key to a healthy relationship lies in finding a place for the remote that is difficult to reach.

The living room is the brain of the house.

If done correctly, it will signal to other organs how to act.

You need to look at your living room from a remote position and look truth straight in the face. Are all family members comfortable there? Is there a bias towards a specific gender? What can be said about you?

You can still do a quick test.

If you have only a sofa in the living room, two armchairs (on both sides of the sofa), a carpet IN FRONT of the sofa, a TV in front and a TV stand underneath it – such a living room can be described as "intolerant" of you and you "should" have a very long conversation about it.

Here are the statements you should "work on":

"But my husband does not need it at all, I do everything I want."

"Nobody even consulted with me!"

"My house reminds me of kindergarten."

"We're really tired at work, and television is the only way to relax."

Everyone who lives in the house should know that the house can entertain him or her at any time, and the living room – as the brain of the house – must give the answer "how".

How to take into account the wishes of EVERYONE? Especially if there are many of them and there's not much space in the living room?

There are baskets, coffee tables, bar tables, walls, after all, console tables and carpets for that.

There IS a place for children's toys in the living room, and they do not need to be constantly taken away and moved to children's rooms.

Of course, it is not necessary to turn the living room into a children's room. It is possible to organize the storage of children's things "in the style of a living room", using sideboards / cupboards / chests / baskets and furniture.

Let's not forget about decor and art.

You definitely can't divide the living room budget only into three equal parts (furniture set – carpet – TV stand), and then "somehow" and "some other time" to buy lamps, interior books, vases, poufs and other decor items.

Let's plan the budget equally. This means that we divide the entire price between all items on the list. And yes, a vase can cost as much as a half of sofa. And yes, that's fine.

A lamp and a sofa cushion can cost more than a TV stand.

And so it will be even much better!

When we see a girl wearing a simple white T-shirt with a Tiffany key on her neck – it does not cause any questions, only admiration. Thus, the IKEA sofa next to the EICHHOLTZ lamps is the Tiffany key on the basic white T-shirt. When in your country you have your own EICHHOLTZ or even better (this is how I felt when I first saw the handmade lamps from @Yedinaceramics_shop in the slab-building technique), then not to take this opportunity would be a crime. Personally, I would replace the lampshades in these lamps, but the basis is a real work of art. That's why you should buy paintings and posters and save on chairs. One interesting item in the living room is enough – another one can be basic.

Let's repeat the key points of gender neutrality in the living room:

- The living room / hall should be the center of your life in the house, in the living room ALL family members should feel at home!

- You do not need to try to eliminate all manifestations of life in it. Do not take children's toys from it, because in the pursuit of tidiness, children will no longer feel their importance and comfort there.

- Think about how you want to spend time there, and provide areas for this. You can dream in the afternoon, play the piano, read, knit, play board games, receive guests, and watch movies. Therefore, everything should be not only beautiful but also functional

- Do not think in terms of "a large item costs a lot, and a small one less." Plan your budget for all furniture and decor items on the list (below) in equal parts.

If you want to update the interior, you do not need to throw away everything you have. You need to get rid of excess. Do not clutter the living room with a lot of random things. You will read more about the fight against clutter in the relevant chapter of this book, but for now, all you need – just fix what you have. If you fill the living room just to fill the void, you will never make it a comfortable nest for everyone.

To make a cool living room, you should:

- Ask each family member what he / she loves and what he / she would like to do in it (or watch this person and you will understand what he / she likes).

- Buy a comfortable sofa and armchairs (not from the one set with the sofa, not the same color as the sofa). Give it a try, please.

- Put an end table / side table / banquette / ottoman / coffee table.

- Refresh the color of the walls to light shades but not the white one in a small room, choose complex and warm colors.

- Pay attention to the "comforters": candles, pillows, wall decor, plaids, unique art objects, family values and chronicles, storage baskets, trays.

- Buy a large carpet (or two) and place all the furniture on it.

- Add flowerpots consciously, not in the way "just to have it".

- Create a visual center. A fireplace would be great, but if you do not have a fireplace – build an artificial one. This center, like a fireplace, can be a picture on the entire wall, a large closet-bar, a projector, a photo gallery on the wall or a huge bookshelf.

- Don't forget about the multi-layering: upholstery, textures, colors, materials.

- Disguise the TV if you use it. What does "disguise" mean? Read more about this in the chapter about TV (although it's high time to replace it with a projector).

- Look at the small living room from a minimalist point of view; make sure it doesn't look crowded. It is a mistake to buy a large sofa in a small living room: it is better to buy a soft carpet, a round table instead of a square one, and large accent paintings on the entire wall!

- Buy one strange item in the living room. How do you know that an object is strange? Just ask 10 people what they think of it. And if 10 of them say it's weird, grab it without thinking. A strange object will always be an occasion for discussion with guests, will take responsibility for removing the inconvenience, but most importantly: despite the humorous form of my story, it is pure truth.

- Add verticals: floor lamps, bookcases and sideboards, columns for sculptures and flasks on them, trees in large pots.

LIST OF PURCHASES FOR THE LIVING ROOM:

(can be crossed out according to size)

- ☐ sofa
- ☐ armchairs, but not from the set (can be replaced by lounge chairs)
- ☐ coffee table / end table / side table / ottoman / banquette
- ☐ side table (not to be confused with the end table)
- ☐ decorative ladder
- ☐ console table or a long drawer standing behind the sofa
- ☐ pictures
- ☐ posters
- ☐ vases
- ☐ interior books
- ☐ trees in pots and houseplants
- ☐ chess board
- ☐ pillows on a sofa
- ☐ plaid
- ☐ carpet
- ☐ floor lamp
- ☐ table lamp
- ☐ aroma diffusers
- ☐ candles
- ☐ tray
- ☐ carafe
- ☐ glass
- ☐ an emphasis on something
- ☐ something old
- ☐ something weird
- ☐ pouf
- ☐ panel picture

You will learn about sofa cushions, the shape of sofas, the location of furniture and why you can't put a sofa against the wall in the relevant chapter. Exhale!

Notes

End table and its variations

End table / side table / coffee table / serving table / console table are all different things.

Each of them without exception is needed in the house, I'm telling you with absolute certainty!

First, they will never be able to "worsen" the look of the room, because they are below eye level.

Secondly, they can instantly make any interior cozy – just put on them a vase of fresh flowers, an interior book or a tray with a carafe and glasses.

Better than such tables can be only two of such tables at different levels.

Decorators use this technique more often than any other, because it is an incredibly easy way to add volume, create multi-layering, and make it look organized and cozy.

In this chapter, we will talk about the varieties of such tables, what and how to put on them.

Composition:

Divide the table into 4 parts, but use only three of them (rule of three).

- At the top right, we put a vase of flowers
- At the bottom left – books in a pile on which you can put a candle
- At the bottom right – an empty space
- At the top left – just one thing (candlestick, sculpture)

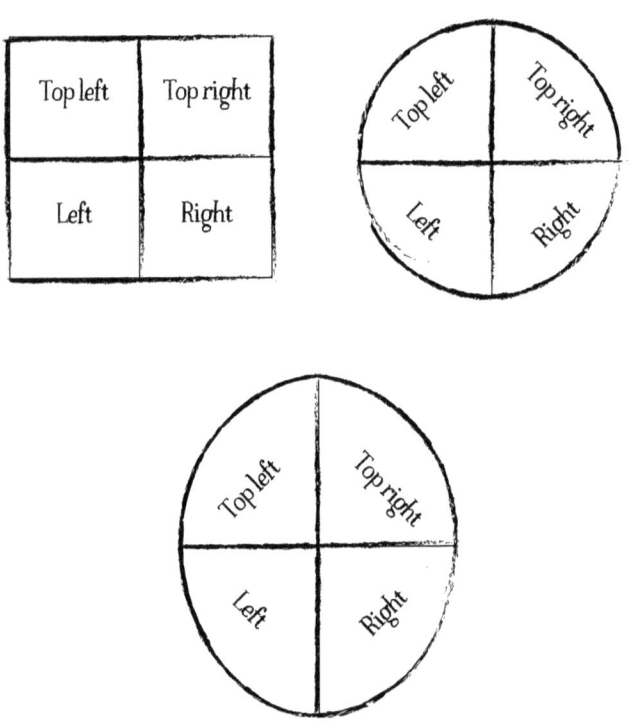

To decorate the table you will need:

- A vase of flowers or a flowerpot / stabilized flowers
- Books (2-3 of them), they will serve as a stand to raise the decor (candles, figurines, vases)
- A candle and matches to it (everything should be functional, we must be able to light a candle)
- A tray (can be on the entire surface of the table or 1/4 of it)
- Anything 30-40 cm in height
- Stone / crystal / piece of wood (something that can be twisted in the hand)
- Decorative box (there we will hide the TV remote control)
- Something individual that reflects your interests today or recent memories

Examples of personal things (found by me in the process of decorating and viewing tons of photos on Pinterest):

- opera glasses
- something vintage for extinguishing a candle
- root
- plastic necklace
- rhino or hippo
- thread balls
- camera
- letter of a name / surname

Along with a long coffee table, you buy many opportunities for self-expression. Do not limit yourself to standard books and flowers, put on it unusual things that represent your secret passions.

Children will need a set of tic-tac-toe games, and a basket made of ice cream sticks will tell others about your abilities, which were amazingly manifested in the summer camp. And let the souvenir from the nearest beach – a snag you found lying on the coastline – proudly lie on the stack of art albums.

TV vs projector

If we describe this whole section concisely in one sentence, it will be:

Communication, but not entertainment!

When we analyze the design projects of Ukrainian design studios, we often see the TV as a central element of the living room. There's no need to complain about the designer, because he is not a customer.

On the contrary, when we analyze the interiors of living rooms in Western Europe and America, we see that the central element of the living rooms are sofas and armchairs, facing each other or the fireplace (fire).

This concept has a very different approach to leisure and spending free time together.

In the first case – entertainment, in the second – communication. Frankly speaking, if families wanted to spend their evenings out of TV, staying in the same living room, they simply couldn't do otherwise! After all, it is necessary to foresee such a possibility.

This way you can't run without sneakers, even if you really want to become an athlete. Turn the sofas and chairs to face each other, put board games on the end table, and books on the side table. Need I remind you that the bar on wheels will easily provide an opportunity to have a drink with your friends or have a tea party?

I'm not here to preach, but I don't want the effort and time you spent on this book and decorating the house to cancel itself out with the appearance of some black rectangle on the wall.

By the way, I really like and watch movies, and this is one of the options for my leisure time, too, but not the only one.

TV is not a universal evil. It's important to attach exactly the significance to TV that it deserves and get the most out of it.

Sometimes the design in the apartment is done "for the cat" (so as not to chew, reach, scratch, eat). It is easy for me to draw a parallel and say that the design of the living room is often done not for people, but for the TV. To make it comfortable, the most beautiful place is chosen and everything else is fitted to it. Nothing revolutionary, everyone has a TV and everyone watches it.

But the TV should never be a central element of space. Disguise it. As if it is in the room, but at the same time as if it is not.

If there is enough space – replace it with a projector. Projector and wall screen are our salvation. It performs the same functions as a TV, but looks much more environmentally friendly: a large canvas in a black frame – a charming friend for any wall. It is a mistake to think that it needs a cinema hall. Modern projectors allow you to look at images from a distance of 2 meters. In addition, they can be laser, portable, handheld, for home cinema. And most importantly – can completely replace the TV.

Here are some less radical tips on how to disguise your TV if you already have one.

1. **Paint the wall on which the TV hangs in a dark color.**

    This wall will help distract attention from the black rectangle.

    You can use hermetic light strips closer to the ceiling, anything that distracts from the black rectangle is welcomed.

    It is **important** that the furniture on this wall was made of light and textured material: wood, painted MDF, rattan cabinets / console tables. Plants, sculptures and various bright colors in the decor will not let you focus on the TV. That's the whole secret.

2. **Shift the focus of attention.**

    TV is not the only object on the wall. Surround it with pictures in black frames and turn on the screen saver in standby mode (like a closed screen on the phone). I saw this screen saver for the first time during a guest visits with Natasha Kalinina – 🅞 nkalinina (a series of videos from different people's homes). It was winter, and there was a screen saver of a burning fireplace with crackling firewood. How wonderful it was! The TV should be part of the overall entourage of the wall gallery.

3. **An analog of the projector Is a panel picture on the entire wall (2x3; 1.8x2.6).**

    If you are not ready to hang paintings or posters, you can hang a large panel picture on the wall. It is appropriate to do this on the gallery hanging system, which is attached to the ceiling. This panel picture can be large. In addition, you have the whole world in your hand – because the canvas is easy to transport.

4. **TV as part of the cabinet.**

   The modular shelving system will also help. Ideally, the TV itself will be closed with a sliding door (sliding system or built-in cabinets). This design will not only hide the TV, but also provide you with such an important additional storage space – you just need to choose the optimal configuration for your space in depth.

5. **Transparent TV from XIAOMI or PANASONIC.**

   If your TV isn't hanging on the wall, but standing in the middle of the living room, then everything is more complicated, but there is always a way out:

   - You can hide it with a folding screen. I've got a beautiful translucent weightless folding screen made of old knitted sweaters – I will recommend it at the end of the book. Such folding screens are also made of thin perforated iron, wood and even mirrors
   - Arrange an oasis near it – lots and lots of greenery. In this case, choose a screen saver in the style of urban jungle or tropical plants.

Sofa and armchairs: no more sets, say yes to accent chairs

You may have a hard time imagining a living room without a sofa and armchairs.

In Guy Ritchie's "The Gentlemen" movie, there is a continuous exhibition hall of the appropriate sofas and decors: chic Chesterfield, aristocratic Tuxedo and cozy Loveseat.

In this chapter, you will learn about the shapes of sofas, sofa cushions, accent chairs and why it is not the best idea to place a sofa against the wall.

Attention!

The main task of this chapter is to acknowledge that you do not need to choose a sofa for the interior! Choose a sofa exclusively for yourself.

I adore leather sofas. I enjoy watching the leather as it is "aging". With proper care, there is nothing more beautiful! It is an ever-changing work of art.

The perfect leather sofa can be both masculine and elegant. Exactly the way I love it. I can imagine it fit in any interior. And I will take it with me to any house.

In general, sofas are quite a significant investment, and therefore it is important to make the right choice.

1. CHOOSE A STYLE FIRST: Do you like chic tufted Chesterfield? Or a more restrained form characteristic of the middle of the century? Scandinavian or classical English? Let's sort it out what sofas are.

Sofas can be roughly divided into several types.

Why roughly? Because there are hundreds of classifications, and we need them only to determine our preferences.

- **CABRIOLE**

    ♥ **Atmosphere:** French living room, sophistication and perfection.

    ★ **Features:** open wooden frame, often with carved figures or ornaments. The backrest smoothly transitions into armrests, which are slightly lower than the base. Comes without back pillows.

    ⊙ **Details:** the legs of the sofa usually resemble the paws of a dog or lion.

- **LAWSON**

    ♥ **Atmosphere:** American lifestyle, comfort and coziness.

    ★ **Features:** three tightly packed pillows on the back and seat. The armrests are a bit lowered and slightly bent. Deep seating.

    ⊙ **Details:** There is a rumor that it was designed for Thomas W. Lawson, a financier and comfort lover, somewhere at the dawn of the 20th century.

- **ENGLISH ROLLED ARM (classic English sofa)**

    ♥ **Atmosphere:** a 1900 British country house.

    ★ **Features:** tight, stiff backrest, small armrests and soft large seat cushions. Short and sturdy legs. Often comes with wheels. The sofa creates a feeling of comfort and relaxation.

    ◉ **Details:** also known as "club sofa".

- **CHESTERFIELD**

    ♥ **Atmosphere:** England, 19th century gentlemen's club.

    ★ **Features:** quilted effect. Low and deep seating. Low rounded backrest with rolled up armrests of the same height. Material – mostly leather. No pillows. Unnoticeable legs.

    ◉ **Details:** supposedly designed so that men can sit up straight, holding their posture, to help keep their suits tidy.

- **CAMELBACK**

    ♥ **Atmosphere:** Classical 18th Century England.

    ★ **Features:** curved back, which rises smoothly to the highest point in the middle and then just as smoothly lowers. It has square armrests of the same height as the back. Sofa comes with exposed legs, no pillows. Elegant and sophisticated.

    ◉ **Details:** Created by Thomas Chippendale, whose name has become synonymous with this period in English home decor.

- **TUXEDO**

    ♥ **Atmosphere:** 1920s modern, chic and glamorous.

    Особливість: high-level armrests with the backrest. Usually has one seat cushion and exposed legs.

    ◉ **Details:** favorite sofa of the decorator Billy Baldwin, designers Jackie O. and Diana Vreeland.

2. LET'S TALK ABOUT COLOR: choose absolutely any, do not try to combine it with curtains and walls color. The sofa is a starting point and the rest of the decor will be selected to match it later: vases, pillows, curtains and other things in the living room. Feel free to choose from emerald green to sapphire blue.

Now when we have figured out the shapes and chosen a sofa to match our liking, it is important to purchase it as a "couple".

The furniture sets are obsolete. Do not buy a set of chairs and sofa.

There is nothing more boring than a set of furniture. In the world of design, there is such a term as "accent chairs". Accent chair is the one that differs from the main sofa with its:

- texture
- ornament
- color

An art object chair can also be considered as an accent chair.

This chair is strikingly contrasting with all and is stunning itself no less than next to its "couple".

Oh yeah! Accent chairs are a true salvation for old and new sofas.

Every sofa needs accent chairs. An armchair not belonging to a complete set with sofa next to it are a Yin and Yang of a living interior.

PLACING THE FURNITURE

The second biggest mistake along the furniture set, I can surely tell you, is the location of the sofa and chairs in a room.

A sofa against the wall and two armchairs by its sides is a layout that is very common in low-income, culturally unsaturated families where watching TV is the only form of pastime. Sometimes a coffee table is placed in the center as well. And the opponent of a person sitting on such a sofa can only be a TV. The first thing I do in this case is a rearrangement.

I want to debunk this "beauty and harmony" myth and ask you not to put a sofa against the wall. Turn the sofa around and face it with the other sofa and armchairs. This will allow you to communicate with your guests.

Move the sofa away from the wall by at least 20-30 cm and set up the console, sideboard, picture, or sculpture!

Even if your living room is not spacious, its size can be balanced by a small sofa and the appropriate accent chairs. Minimalistic carpet may help it as well. But the rule "do not place it against the wall" works for all rooms without exception.

AND WHAT DO WE PLACE AGAINST THE WALL?

You may consider a high table-console to place against the wall. The console can be 20-25 cm deep. This table creates that cherished "multi-layered" effect. The additional console area will allow you to place a medium light source, which adds comfort; books and other personalized items for your living room will serve as a stand for a cup of tea / fruit plate and other things. It may well replace the side table if the room is small.

What else can be placed against the wall?

1. Shelving unit, wooden columns, shelves, plants and anything you want. The main rule states: this "anything" should be on a higher level than the sofa.
2. To put, or not to put? You can definitely hang or put it on the floor.
3. A picture the size of a sofa. Leave the manners aside! You chose a "dare", so go for it.

The third mistake I would like to mention is sewing sofa pillows from curtain material.

We do not sew pillows to match the color of curtains; it is a **taboo**! And do not even touch the residual materials!

Fortunately, we do have taste and imagination. It is not a stylish way to follow. And it seriously lacks coziness. Besides, interesting pillow designs are the most amazing and inexpensive way to update once a season, add comfort and colors in a matter of minutes.

Our market is filled with the most interesting offers. The full list of manufacturers that I have mentioned in my shortlist, I will share at the end of the book. I can say that we have Ukrainian Gucci – 📷 dotuk_story, as well as incredible 📷 yasykdeco and their modern ethnic motifs in their best interpretation.

Of course, I also love the "old-timers" of the world's pillow manufacturers. Among them, I can recommend www.designersguild.com. I advise you to check it at least for inspiration and to understand how things can be arranged.

A simple **life hack**: print a picture of your child on the fabric and make a pillowcase. It looks very beautiful even in the strictest living room (but after the chapter on the living room and its inhabitants, I hope it is no longer the perfection?).

LET'S TALK ABOUT THE QUANTITY

A bunch of different pillows will not add to comfort.

Just as with a table setting, there is a certain rhythm to the sofa. In order to avoid overload, keep in mind the appropriate number of pillows.

- Sofa for two – 3 pillows (2 on the right and 1 on the left)
- Classic sofa – 4 pillows (2 on the right + 2 on the left)
- Large sofa – 5 pillows (2 on the right + 1 in the center + 2 on the left)
- Corner sofa – 7 pillows (2 at the edges and 3 in the corner).

They all can differ in shape and size. We put larger pillows at the back and smaller ones at the front. An interesting "solo" shape.

It wouldn't be me if I didn't pay attention to a small detail that spoils the cozy sofa look – remote controls.

REMOTE CONTROLS

If you often lose your remote controls, the book Remodelista offers an option for convenient storage. A bag-organizer with pockets attached to the handle of the sofa is enough. Store your remotes there and cover it with a blanket.

Notes

#bringmerugs

I love rugs dearly. If you don't like them, it's only a matter of time before you will after reading this chapter. The ability to learn how to communicate with them is similar to the maternal instinct – you only have to wake it up!

"To irrevocably become a rug maniac, it is enough to enter the word 'rug' on Pinterest," said Anna Kalenska, the owner of the agency for the selection of nannies and mother of 4 children at the marathon of visual experience. And she was right!

If you have time to spend a few hours on the Internet – then look for these names:

1. LRNCE by Laurence Leenaert – lifestyle carpets from Marrakech by a Belgian designer who specializes in interior decoration and accessories. She conquers the world by revising the purpose of materials and spontaneously combining textiles with hemp, clay, sisal, and leather and creating products with unique designs. According to art expert Larysa Tsybin, "connoisseurs of such emotional objects do not concentrate in European cities; or rather they are Europeans who do NOT live in cities. These are relaxed celebrities on the islands and in the Marrakech riads, these are hedonists on the coasts, in houses open to the sun and winds. These are mountains and mists in the morning and a camel rug under feet. Such items need an atmosphere, and if they get there, it turns out to be a small paradise."

2. Faig Ahmed is an Azerbaijani artist who takes huge, beautiful, complex Azerbaijani carpets, rips them open, and gives the carpets a new look using optical techniques and techniques that resemble elements of Modern Art. I admire his talent for remaking the old into the new, allowing the object to be displayed in galleries as a work of art.

3. Kustaa Saksi is a Finnish artist and designer from Amsterdam. He specializes in graphic storytelling through patterns, textile art, and installation. He suffers from hypnopompic hallucinations – these are visual, tactile, sound, or other sensory events, usually short but sometimes prolonged, that occur during the transition from sleep to activity. His rugs are his visions.

4. Edward Barber and Jay Osgerby are a British design duo from London, known for their innovative interiors and industrial design. They designed the Olympic flame in London in 2012, and their work is in many permanent collections around the world. Their collection for The Rug Company is fun, colorful, and playful.

5. ANN Cathrin NOVEMBER. Of course, if I could name my favorite item in the house – it would be it!

But in this relationship, I am polygamous. I don't have any favorites.

I've already looked for a transparent wooden rack for them. And I'll put it in the most visible place. The ends of completely different rugs from all over the world will look at me, and when my eyes stop at any of them, I will mentally travel. I get goose bumps at the thought, and so should you. No, goose bumps come from the rugs themselves. They happen when you really find something that "grabs" you.

It's not just art that can "grab you", although this is its direct purpose. Every item in the house can be art – from cups to blankets. And a rug can be an art form. The people I just mentioned are a vivid confirmation of this. I only have such items in my home. When I found Marina 📷 pupcha_kilim, I knew it at first glance. My house was waiting for her exclusive prints with incredible colors. With them, the already not boring house became truly cozy and complete.

RUG GUIDE

It is quite clear that rugs are different. In this book, I'll take you through the ones that, in my opinion, are timeless.

My list includes wool, cotton, silk, and straw rugs. But hemp, clay, sisal, and leather carpets are also an option. The material is primary.

The rug can't be acrylic, unnatural and heavy. Only an EXPENSIVE Persian silk rug can be heavy.

On the contrary, even the largest rugs should be easy to fold.

Here are some "rug countries":

Egypt, Sweden, Denmark, Germany, Morocco, Georgia, Armenia, Azerbaijan, Belgium, Finland, India, Nepal, USA, Turkey, UAE, and Iran.

Each of these has its own wonderful rugs because the traditions of their weaving are passed down from generation to generation.

Try to find time to look for these names for inspiration.

UKRAINE:

- pupcha_kilim
- oksana_levchenya
- ivanka_carpet
- kilimartstudio
- Gushka.wool
- oshainua
- zvyazani
- oleziolezi

WORLD:

- vanessabarragao_work
- cc_tapis
- nanimarquina_official
- Jasonseife
- lrnce
- nexthomecollection
- kustaasaksi
- anthropologie
- _jujujust_
- rosepearlman
- laformahome
- doinggoods
- allyrous

Where to buy vintage rugs and authentic rugs?

The most beautiful and best finds I bought:
- at flea markets
- on repeat sales sites (for example Marktpatz, eBay)
- from niche local producers – 🅾 pupcha.kilim

In interiors, the size of the rug is also important. A rug can unite a space into a single ensemble – it works as a tray for small details. A table and a quartet of chairs, a sofa and armchairs with a coffee table, a bed and a bench at the foot of the bed – all this is impossible to imagine without a background in the form of a rug. You need to choose such a size that all of the above can be easily placed on top of it. From the very moment you set foot on the rug or your eyes stop at an unusual pattern, you will feel at home.

Life hack #1

Since I write about thin rugs that are easy to store and clean, I sometimes lack the softness underneath. It is worth putting a memory foam lining under the rug (it can be a simple mattress pad made of this material) – and your life will never be the same again. Incredible softness and comfort will become your daily companions.

Life hack #2

If the floor is made of natural wood, wool rugs often slide on it. Therefore, put special pads under them. In IKEA, they are called rug and carpet underlays.

MULTI-LAYERED CARPETS

Bright carpets of unusual colors are often small in size.

This is not a reason not to use them in large rooms, for example, in the living room. Buy a basic carpet made of cotton or straw in beige or gray color of large size (these are sold in IKEA), and put colored carpets of different shapes and sizes on top of it.

GRANDMOTHER'S RUGS

The rugs on the walls don't look as terrible as we remember.

I often hang rugs on the wall, just take very thin ones and stretch them on a stretcher in baguette workshops. This is a great alternative to posters and paintings. Especially when some are even scary to walk on.

This technique appeared in my arsenal completely by accident.

I once bought such a rug on the OLX website: it was a hand-embroidered cross-stitch of 1.3 x 3 size. Since there are children in the house, I knew that this rug would not be on the floor for more than a year. It had gaps of 6 cm on each side (apparently designed for an anti-slip lining), and I framed it in a stretcher and hung it on the wall. In just a few months, it had "overgrown" with a chess table and chairs that perfectly matched it. Before this rug appeared, I would never have thought of putting a table there: this is what the right things do to space in the right place. They decorate themselves.

Rugs are incredibly practical: you can take them to a photo shoot (put the rug just on the grass-and bohemian pictures are guaranteed!)

That's exactly where you shouldn't bother about the brand, so it's when choosing rugs. But to navigate the sites of repeat sales and niche manufacturers, you need to familiarize yourself with the icons of carpet style. Visual experience has not been canceled, so be sure to review the works of art by those authors and brands that I mentioned at the beginning of the chapter.

Photos in the house

It is hard to find more cozy and warm elements for the house. Especially if they were created by you or your loved ones.

Here are some tricks on why you need to have photos in the house and how to match them with the interior.

CHILDREN

Photos for children create a feeling of security. Children understand the importance of family and are proud of it; they are pleased with the memories.

There should be at least 2-3 photos in the children's room. For example, a photo of children's achievements, family photos, and photos of the parents' successes.

For instance, with the help of photos in his room, I try to instill in Sasha, my middle child, the love of sports.

We have a photo from the swimming competition in "Ocean Kids", which, in fact, was not easy for him; his father's ascent of the mountain – he talks to him a lot about the mountains and hiking. Also, there is an old photograph of runners, bought on the Andriyivskyy Descent.

The main thing is not to emphasize the photos, but to put them near the things that the child uses: a toy shelf, bed, and desk. I arrange photos near the vases, which partially cover the image, and we create the natural look that we need. This is the parental trick.

ADULTS

It is better to place a large number of photos in the same frames, arranging themeither where you spend time together or in the areas pass through: living room, hallway, or kitchen.

The Japanese culture method works well here, where broken spruce emphasizes the perfection of the rest of the forest. For example, 4 identical square frames and 1 oval, round or antique – which is not like the others. But in strict order.

RELATIVES AND FRIENDS

It's a good idea to have photos of other family members; they can be placed on the same large photo wall.

Friends are family we choose ourselves. A place in your home equals a place in your heart.

RECOMMENDATIONS

Do not forget that photo frames get outdated quickly, so you should replace them with new ones from time to time.

Today black and white laconic frames in the Stockholm style are relevant for the color photos. Black and white photos are grouped together in a wooden frame. The more interesting the photo is, the simpler the frame should be.

Homework:

Replace the outdated frames with more modern ones.

Books and bookshelves in the house

The whole world is divided into two camps: some read only e-books and consider paper books to be a relic of the past, others cannot imagine a cozy house without at least a few books, and even bookshelves, where they can find their favorite copies.

If you are reading this book, we are most likely in the same boat.

Well, I will move over, and you may sit more comfortably.

Remember about the balance. There should not be many books, and if your grandmother's collection occupies half of the apartment, it is worth finding a temporary shelter for them.

However, even a small one-room apartment may be decorated with several bookshelves. There are several rules for the design of bookshelves:

1. Many people like to arrange books by color, and I'm no exception. The main thing is to arrange them on the open shelves, with the obligatory presence of all colors. It is good if there is a third object (a chair, an armchair, a rug), which will match with the color at the level of our eyes.

2. Mix colored objects with books of the same color.

3. Add a few massive things, so self-sufficient, that they will take one's eyes off a number of books.

4. Use pictures with books.

5. Catalog books by topic and sign each of them.

I really like the so-called coffee table books – gift books and photo books. You can just flick through them instead of reading them and they are a good source of training the visual experience. You can flick through them for at least 5 minutes a day over a cup of tea.

These can be hobby books, because their main advantage is that you can open them on any page, and you do not need to read the text, because 80% of such books consist of pictures.

Homework:

Add the following books to your library:

- "The Story of Design", Charlotte Fiell, Peter Fiell
- "Great Designs", Philip Wilkinson
- "Modern Furniture: 150 Years of Design", Volker Albus
- "100 Midcentury Chairs: And Their Stories", Lucy Richardson
- "Hans J. Wegner: Just One Good Chair", Christian Olesen
- several books by Assouline publishing house, especially pink "IBIZA"
- any of Helmut Newton's books

Makeover and decluttering – a permanent process of any cozy home

I'm not a wardrobe specialist, but I understand something about homes.

The Swedes introduced the term Dostadning, which means "death cleaning." Its author is Margareta Magnusson, a mother of five, which undoubtedly gives her a great deal of experience in eliminating all kinds of clutter.

The feeling when your house is cluttered is the same as when you are getting sick – nothing makes you happy anymore: not new things, not even your favorite movie.

The only cure is a time to "be down with the flu" and relax, think – unclutter. Why time? Because it's not a matter of one weekend, but rather an ongoing process. Spring-cleaning is not in trend now – preventive cleaning "runs" everything. But how to do it when you don't even know how many cups for tea, pans, napkins, books you have?

The first rule of decluttering is the realization that we don't need so many things.

You start to feel overwhelmed with clutter when you hardly find the right thing in a pile of "just things", and everything that catches your eye is something you don't love anymore.

Decluttering is not about minimalism, no.

Decluttering is about the air you want to breathe, about comfort, about empty shelves in the closet. It means that the inside should be more beautiful than the outside, and that goes for everything.

I really like the Japanese saying: "fast is slow, but every day".

The most painful issue of every home of my clients, without exception, was the absurdly large number of things in their life. We have become hostages to our own things and we constantly serve them. We are attached to them and put off living in order to buy them. We feel attached to them, but the best things in life are not things at all. We do not know where to put them, and mistakenly believe that if we hide them in the closet, they won't bother us until someday we will need them. But of course, they will bother us!

Every interior should "push" to some action. You must want to come in; to be in it (sit down, lie down); act in it (put your feet in your slippers, take off your clothes); be inspired by it. Otherwise – what is its purpose?

I'm afraid of skewing in either direction, "+" or "–". Here and there, there is a chance to lose the sense of reality, to start thinking that you are just a grain of sand, or, conversely, to feel like the king of the mountain, as in the children's game.

Clutter interferes with our attention to details, dulls the understanding that color and shape can change everything, especially the desire to be and live in a beautiful environment always and everywhere.

One of the secrets of my house is its constant makeover and getting rid of clutter.

This is a permanent process.

This aesthetic of everyday life can be introduced by applying the following habits:

1. EVERY DAY I TAKE AWAY 15 THINGS FROM THE HOUSE

It seems a little over the top, but in fact, I do not throw them in the trash. They just need new hosts or applications. These could be broken or small things, things that I almost never use.

Such things take up space; create visual noise – the main enemy of a good home.

If I have not had feeling for things for a long time, I say goodbye to them easily. Every time I feel strongly attached to something, I part with it:

- first, things are made for joy, not for us to serve them and become their slaves
- second, it allows us to reach new levels, not to get hung up and not to stay in the comfort zone. It is very important to me that the house remains a place of strength and meets the interests of current reality, gives residents a sense of peace, but I am a living person and always buy something.

If you compare this ideology with food, then in order not to count the number of berries and not to weigh every gram of food, you just need to do sports and lead an active lifestyle.

2. EVERY WEEK I BUY SOMETHING FROM DECOR

This is super important, because with the classic renovation and the choice of canonical things that do not go out of fashion, we risk living in a house deprived of ourselves. Such things definitely have a right to exist; you just need to remember the balance. Such a decor cannot be bought at one time, given its cost and the time it takes.

So, every week I buy decor:

- from local producers
- on decor and furniture websites (Markplatz, kringloop)
- at flea markets
- at auctions (like eBay)

I do it during the week as well as on the weekends, and I try to "insert" purchased items into already available home decor. Before you ask, I'll tell you that it doesn't always work out, it doesn't always work out well, but once a month a diamond comes out.

I set myself a limit of UAH 1,000 per week for such things, which is the same amount I donate to charity and creative growth. I just tell myself that the people who sell them are in need of money more; to support their business, for life and just to encourage them. I always, if possible, send photos of "purchases" in the interior to sellers. Small talk is a powerful weapon, please use it.

Of course, sometimes I do not fit into the budget, but for me there is nothing better than limited opportunities. Restrictions only feed the creativity.

I really liked one of my followers' phrase on the social network:

"A complex subject line makes the interior deep, multi-layered, creates a sense of home with history. It is as if rooms have evolved over time, without designer intervention. And that's the highest level of skill".

I would add that such multi-layered effect cannot be achieved without weekly work, risk, and trial and error.

We are now in an era of overconsumption. We learn to part with things, and rightly so. You don't have to build relationships with things, you have to build them with people.

Things give us a false sense of fulfillment, but in reality, we only stimulate our brain to buy more and more, thus producing dopamine. Why put off living for a new TV? In fact, we do not need it at all.

3. MONTHLY I BUY SOME COLLECTOR'S ITEMS

Yesterday, for example, I opened a book about the Trehubovs (a husband and wife who worked at the Korosten Porcelain Factory) and then on OLX I looked for what I liked. Notably, sellers are often unaware of what treasure they are selling. The most they know is the name of the factory.

Informed means armed. I search for "porcelain", "cups" and put Korosten as geolocation. After that, my collection was enlarged with 2 cups, one vase and one decanter. And why am I not a collector? Collecting is not suitable for digitals, read about them in the chapter "4 types of perceiving information."

To collect is to pay attention to oneself, let's call it "to please oneself". There will be a separate chapter on collecting, but for now, I suggest you make a wish list for birthdays and other holidays.

I would like to raise this topic in this chapter, because gifts are an essential part of clutter in our lives. We are often given something unnecessary. Because of love for friends, relatives and loved ones, we live with these gifts and are afraid to throw them away so as not to offend them. Sounds familiar?

In this regard, I will tell you the story of one couple.

The lovely couple used to live in love and respect all their lives up to their silver wedding.

In the evening, during dinner, the wife cuts off a heel of bread, spreads butter on it and at the same time thinks: "Well, at least today I can afford the end-piece, and then all my life I gave it to my husband!" The man notices this and joyfully announces: "Finally you've eaten the top crust yourself! I don't love them so much and I've eaten them all these years just so as not to offend you, because you gave them to me!"

What can we say about the loved ones who have been trying to please you all their lives by giving you random meaningless gifts? You would help them a lot by making a wish list of necessary or desired things. Then there would be much less unnecessary things in the house, and you would not have to think about what to do with them.

Such a wish list can be of home touch points, everyday items or the ones "with a claim to art".

I can share my own, maybe it will inspire you to create your own.

It will also come in handy when you need to get a gift for someone creative.

MY WISH LIST FOR MANY YEARS HAS BEEN AS FOLLOWS:

- bird feeder Eva solo
- flowerpot hay
- water carafe hay, LSA
- organizer for cutlery MOOD BY CHRISTOFLE
- copper tray mauviel
- vase Mutto / Sofika ceramics
- dunoon cups
- vintage champagne bucket
- candlesticks pols potten
- Jamie Hayon vase
- glasses nasonmotetti
- posters sonic edition
- interior books assouline / tashen / skira
- carafe raawii
- Tom Dixon coffee set
- Jo Malone candles / venini / ca'venezia
- candlesticks Norman Copenhagen
- plates of labarotoria paravicini

You will find a list of decor stores in the relevant chapter of this book – there you will find where to break loose and what to want for many years. Remember – shopping should be done consciously.

4. EVERY SIX MONTHS I DO A MAKEOVER OF THE HOUSE: change paintings, move furniture (if possible, of course), even if everything satisfies me.

It helps to:

- make sure you have made the right planning decision
- refresh the house

- master your skills
- look over the unnecessary things and get rid of something you haven't used for 6 months or forever
- find a new look at old things, because they are perceived differently in different places.

5. EVERY YEAR I DO THE "DEATH" CLEANING OF THE HOUSE

I sit down, make delicious tea and describe my way of life and the way of life for my children or those that we aspire to. Next – check the compass. Does my house fit this path?

I add zones and change the functionality of rooms. Yes, you can bring a desk to the first-grader's room, review the organization of toys, and add a sports area to your room, change the purpose of the office, living room, and library – the main thing is that they meet your needs today.

FOCUS ON THE MAIN THING OR QUARANTINE OF CONSUMPTION

Li Edelkoort (trendtablet.com) says that COVID-19 will help us remove everything superfluous, instilled by the accelerated pace of life, and trust what nature tells us. It will help to restore the main simple values in the memory and in the houses and to rebuild them.

Recall the activities we already have and those that we forgot about, whether it's reading a book or cooking dinner, board games or reading together with the family, crocheting and drawing (the list is not exhaustive). In fact, this is all that we got around to or did not have enough time for it. All that can make us happy and the house cozy.

Let's try to use this as an opportunity.

I urge you not to be a maximalist, not to look for the perfect table or bar, dresser or chair. Less is more.

Think about such activities and create such an island of joy at home. Maybe you need to add quite a bit or maybe you just need to start using it. It's time to clean up and focus on your happiness in the best home clothes.

> **Tip:** involve children in decluttering and tidying up in the area of their responsibility – their room

No cleaning marathon, knowledge of design and decor and training CAN BE APPLIED on the old foundation without new energy.

For me, order in the house is order in the mind. And it can't be any other way.

Below there is a list of books and resources if you are ready to dive into it:

BOOKS:

1. "The Complete Book of Home Organization": (Hammersley Toni).
2. "A Monk's Guide to a Clean House and Mind" (Shoukei Matsumoto).
3. "The Life-Changing Magic of Tidying: A simple, effective way to banish clutter forever" (Marie Kondo).
4. "Spark Joy: An Illustrated Master Class on the Art of Organizing and Tidying Up" (Marie Kondo).
5. "Breathing Room. Open Your Heart by Decluttering Your Home" (Lauren Rosenfeld).
6. "Step Out of Your Old Shoes!: Let Go of Old Habits Give Your Life New Direction" (Robert Betz).
7. "The 8 Minute Organizer: Easy Solutions to Simplify Your Life in Your Spare Time" (Regina Leeds).
8. "The Zen of Organizing. Creating Order and Peace in Your Home, Career and Life" (Regina Leeds).
9. "Never Too Busy to Cure Clutter: Simplify Your Life One Minute at a Time" (Erin Rooney Doland).
10. "The Joy of LessA Minimalist Guide to Declutter, Organize, and Simplify" (Francine Jay).
11. "Sink Reflections: FlyLady's BabyStep Guide to Overcoming CHAOS" (Marla Cilley).
12. "Decluttering at the Speed of Life: Winning Your Never-Ending Battle with Stuff" (Dana K. White).
13. "The Gentle Art of Swedish Death Cleaning" (Margareta Magnusson).

14. "The art of living is simple. How to get rid of excess and enrich your life" (Dominic Loro).
15. Remodelista. The Organized Home (Margot Guralnick, Julie Carlson).

Instagram-inspiration:

- home_feyka
- ergonomic.girl
- poryadok.v.dome_
- vremya.poryadka
- anna.annyday
- alinasilver

But remember one thing: all this knowledge must stand on a solid foundation, the key to which is saying "no" to excesses in your life.

Life is too good to be content with mediocre life. Choose the best.

Notes

Plants and flowers

Up until this point, I underestimated houseplants.

But, just as with music and my favorite movies, my life was divided into "before" and "after" the discovery of their importance. The experience of the Soviet Union and my family did not allow me to fully appreciate the beauty of houseplants, until the Internet brought me to the incredible bloggers, whose lives were filled with completely different plants than I ever knew existed, and at the same time, I looked at them differently.

Here is a list of my favorite bloggers, their posts and photos motivate me to plunge into the incredible atmosphere of the green kingdom:

- urbanjungleblog
- igorjosif
- joelixjoelix

While following them, I came across the hashtag #urbanjungle

And I fell in love!!!

Urban jungle is an incredible color and texture of plants, harmony with nature and continuous meditation.

The main thing I saw was a competent composition of colors, shapes, sizes and textures. You don't have to be a florist to notice the amazing things that nature has created: just imagine the marble patterns of the leaves combined with the smooth shiny ones!

Since then, life has forced me to notice them everywhere: in the grocery store, I paid attention to the department with live plants, and sometimes there were very unusual specimens; while enjoying coffee in my favorite restaurant, I was watching huge olives; when I came to the new hotel, I was fascinated by the integration of landscape gardening and plants inside.

Scientists call this effect the Baader-Meinhof phenomenon – a cognitive bias in which, after noticing something for the first time, there is a tendency to notice it more often, leading someone to believe that it has a high frequency of occurrence.

Later, when I had the opportunity to find incredible plants, I combined them with those I already had, put them all together, and then one by one took away the flowers that did not fit well into the "company" of the others. As a result, I got a well-built composition with one visual center. This center could be, in fact, the dominant plant itself, or, for example, an unusual pot or a bright decor item. Over time, as my skills and experience grew, I created "family portraits" of plants, jokingly choosing nicknames and adding "children".

Another version of the "family portrait" – several plants of the same species. Just separate the young sprouts by putting them in smaller pots and put the "kids" next to the "mom".

I placed such compositions on all possible surfaces, and my already cozy house – brightened up!

Exactly!

Plants are full-fledged elements in the interior, as well as other furniture: just look – cacti and succulents look like living sculptures, and ivy is the perfect background for a photo, a large Mexican cactus befriended with picture of Frieda, singing an ode to Mexican cushions on a chair!

Now I have a manifesto to decorate the house with plants (it is the original plan for greening), and I want to share it:

1. The style of your home should play in unison with the plants that grow in it, not conflict with them.
2. Plants perform many functions, in addition to air purification (see below).
3. Create plants compositions without experiencing the impostor syndrome.
4. Take care of them, because there is nothing worse than dying plants in the house.

HOUSE STYLE AND PLANTS

The style of plants should be integrated into the overall interior, not contradict it.

For example, my house is completely eclectic, so I find a lot of cute pots at flea markets and combine them with modern ones. Antique coffee and teacups, copper cachepots are great containers for small plants. Since I am 50% digital, I choose plants by symbols: so I have in my house a flower of love (shamrock), a prayer flower (calathea) and a Chinese money tree.

I adore the botanical theme. On the facades of the furniture or its interior, I use fabric or remnants of floral wallpaper purchased in vintage stores, or, as we did with Lilith Sarkisian ⓘ litsarkisian (goddess of floral walls) – just painted a floral fragment on an old dresser, and it was stunning!

Do not forget about the functions of plants (except that they clean the air). They can create comfort and add accents. Here's how you can use plants to:

- turn a bath into a spa by adding ferns and Aloe Vera, they can be placed directly on the bath shelf – this is my favorite trick, you are welcome to use it!
- in the home office (on the desktop) you can create an incredible atmosphere of creativity if you add ceramic or knitted relatives to plants, such as cacti.
- in the living room with the help of plants you can create an atmosphere of calm and relaxation, or, conversely, gaming! As well as a space zoning.
- in the bedroom you can create the atmosphere of wildlife in the woods and recover after a long working day.
- in the children's room plants can complement any "theme", as a bonus is instilling in even the youngest child responsibility and organization: just buy her a watering can and ask to take care of the plant.

Create compositions from plants without feeling like an impostor. I like to answer this: who will judge you?

But if you are still a little scared, I will give you the basics of composition and the examples of decorating with plants below, as well as my personal "no" in decorating the house with plants:

Let's start with the "No" list:

- ✗ plants on the floor (exceptions only confirm the rules, so sometimes large plants in very, very beautiful pots can be on the floor!)
- ✗ half-dead plants
- ✗ plants on windowsills
- ✗ plants standing alone without compositions
- ✗ plants that are put to hide some "snag" in the house
- ✗ plants that were given to you, but you do not like them.

And now the "Yes" list:

- decoration with plants has the best effect if it is built around a certain theme, and only then, decor is added
- large houseplants like to be alone, but then the pot for such a plant is an equal participant in the composition + add a small decor next to it

- plants are selected to fit the pots, not the place so that they can travel safely throughout your home, from composition to composition
- I can tell to connoisseurs of minimalism – pay attention to bonsai: a couple of such well-located plants will enliven the interior.

A FEW WORDS ABOUT CACHEPOTS / POTS:

When you are making a composition, a variety of flowerpots (for example, vintage, retro and modern) in one color works great (different shades are allowed). This will give the composition a certain integrity.

I also suggest "breaking bad" and collect all the variety of such pots, but provided that it will be really a variety, not just pots of different colors.

> **Tip:** start with combining cacti with vintage items that you have no use for.

If you want to decorate the piano with plants, take pots without drainage holes and those that do not like water. And put them on the books on one side of the piano, and a large vase on the other side for balance.

I do not like flowers on the floor. Use any plant stands. In fact, it can be everything that has a small flat area – the more unusual, the better: stools, ladders, suitcases, benches and everything that has a horizontal surface.

> **Tip:** children's furniture from the flea market will fit perfectly in size as a stand for plants, even in a small apartment.

Don't worry if you bought a cache-pot at the flea market without a plate, it can easily be made by painting vintage plates in gold or silver. If you do not have time to visit the flea market, vintage pots and brass rose bowls can be purchased at 📷 vintage.antique.kiev or 📷 marmur.studio, while sitting on the couch at home

PLANT CARE

I emphasize once again: there is nothing worse than a dying flower.

The house will look untidy and uncared for when flowers die in it. In addition, they stop to perform their functions – dust clogs the holes through which plants exhale oxygen and inhale carbon dioxide, and their ability to purify the air decreases sharply. Other functions are also difficult to perform when you are dying.

At the very beginning of your journey, this is a very possible scenario. So if you do not have experience, choose unpretentious flowers (you will find a list of such at the end of the chapter).

Don't force yourself – plants should please you, so choose the ones that best suit your lifestyle.

If the plant has died – this is merely a reason to choose a new one, but not to give up.

It is difficult for me to write about the care for each individual plant, and it is not necessary: you can easily find it online. Here I want to tell you how to turn caring for them into a ritual, where routine gives you energy, rather than take it away.

Caring for plants can be a daily ritual and a personal timeout – if you look at it from this angle. Caring for plants is much more interesting if you have nice tools. Buy a designer watering can (preferably several for different parts of the house), a beautiful pair of secateurs and an interesting water spray. Make yourself a photo shoot; care can be inspiring.

You are probably wondering what plants have settled in my house:

1. I prefer a large olive tree to a large ficus or palm tree. The olive tree is what takes me on vacation, even if I'm slicing a salad in the kitchen.

2. I once read that if you could turn a swarm of purple butterflies into a plant, it would become triangular shamrock. After that, I settled 5 such plants – it is called the flower of love! I was captivated by the fact that the flower of love can be eaten. Both leaves and flowers are edible raw or cooked. They have a fruity, sour taste. This is a very fitting and good addition to a salad. In fact, it is a decorative sorrel.

3. I am 50% digital, so when I heard about the prayer flower – calathea – I immediately bought it. The pattern on its leaves looks like a million small leaves.

4. Chinese money tree – pilea peperomioides – a real star of botanical bloggers. It is adored by Scandinavians, and for some reason by me.
5. Another resident of my house is a snake plant (sansevieria). I love it for being so !!! easy to care for. This succulent stores water and can live even in hard to reach and dark places, such as the laundry room or toilet. If it could be stored in the refrigerator – I would do it, I also love that it was beautiful there.
6. I also have Aloe Vera, it was once given to me as a starter kit for beginners, it is very useful and easy to care for.

I am happy to share a list for beginners:

- spathiphyllum
- epipremnum
- snake plant
- chlorophytum
- aloe vera

If this topic turned out to be super interesting for you, I suggest you dive into the world of not boring, wonderful books with a million inspiring photos:

- 📷 planttribebook
- "Urban Jungle: Living and Styling with Plants" (Igor Josifovic, Judith de Graaff)
- "PLANT TRIBE – Living happily ever after with Plants" (Igor Josifovic, Judith de Graaff)

Fresh flowers in the house, or promise to give yourself flowers and this will change your life

The Swedes have the concept of "Friday bouquet". Every Friday they buy a bouquet of fresh flowers for their house. The French and Italians have the same practice, and they are certainly the experts in the pleasure of life.

Living with flowers is an opportunity to live in the moment and fully enjoy it. Opportunity to stop. Absolutely any house is personated with flowers in it. Make your home a sacred place. The girl really needs fresh flowers. The point is not so in flowers themselves as in the metamorphosis that will happen to you when you start dealing with them. It is a connection with nature and self-awareness.

One of my subscribers, Zhenia Yordanova, started practicing #flowersasabasicneed and here is what she said after 6 months of buying flowers every day:

#flowersasabasicneed is a study of my personal history, which dates back to my childhood.

"Cashmere sweater is expensive, acrylic is no worse, and it lasts longer… "

"Expensive perfume is too expensive, on tap is the same; you can't tell the difference…"

"Face mask is expensive, cucumber is better. While chopping salad, rub cucumber on your face."

"Bouquets in the store – expensive, we have beautiful flowers in the garden. In winter? How long is that winter?!"

I am an adult, independent, financially independent. I'm afraid of expensive shops, beauty salons and floral boutiques. I buy very expensive bouquets just for someone. For myself – rarely, almost never. The fear of "it's expensive" is deeply rooted in me. But life is an interesting thing. One day I find myself in a completely new city, in a completely new life, where I can get a fresh start without losing previous life experience. Practically "Jumanji".

At first, I worked in a boutique of Dutch florists, getting to know the inner world of expensive bouquets. I learned how to create flower arrangements using "floral wire". Since then I have been dearly loving flowers and we have been friends with them. And most importantly – I'm not afraid of them.

Then I received an invitation to work in the most expensive clothing and footwear boutique in the city. I immersed myself in this environment and now I am not afraid of luxurious designer interiors, staff's appreciative glances, cashmere sweaters, silk blouses, gorgeous shoes.

Having analyzed my experience, I can say that the quality of our lives depends only on ourselves. Be sure to try both acrylic sweater and cashmere. Buy yourself a very expensive bouquet or even a bouquet of wildflowers while jogging, only for yourself. Do only what you personally like; listen to yourself, not to the voices from childhood.

Fresh flowers in the house are something I personally like. Heartiness, tenderness and calmth.

If I think that it is time to replace the bouquet, it means – harmony in my universe, and I can afford the luxury of thinking about flowers and mentally choose a vase. Quality of life is a ritual of self-love."

I completely agree with Zhenia.

Everything is much deeper. Now many florists, from small to large, promote flowers for every day. This is almost the only propaganda for good!

It is not about popular "flowers in the house", but about getting into a habit of making your everyday life beautiful with your own hands.

This is the first stage of a real contract with yourself and the implementation of the habit of creating beauty. The beauty of everyday life is the least you can afford right now, despite of all financial situations.

The purchase of flowers for home involves the exchange of energy with sellers, a small talk with a person who faces the beauty every day, and about the long life of these flowers in your home (the bouquet will change every few days).

Just order flowers every week or as they wither.

Now is a magical time for this habit: there are florists everywhere: in every supermarket, the elderly women on the way home, in the subway and in the market, floral farms with home delivery.

Realize your preferences and tastes. Ask yourself what kind of flower you are.

I adore flowers, especially peonies! When I made the challenge #nodaywithoutpeonies, I had no idea how much I loved them. Goosebumps. My husband, as it turned out, hadn't known that I loved them. I am 100% peony. Each time it is unique – and of such stunning shades that no one has ever seen before, with an incredible smell. Those people who have made an effort and flowers became the part of their normal rhythm of life will never backtrack. It's like discovering music, movies, literature or traveling and all the things you can't imagine your life without if they're already with you. This is also art. Flowers are paintings, not painted, but alive.

Flowers take your life to a whole new level, believe me.

After all, your own home is an opportunity to unite in one place everything that you love or could love.

One of my friends told me about her experiment. It was an experiment in self-discipline. After a month of buying flowers every day, it seemed to her that nothing had changed, but the promise was made and every 6-7 days she always bought herself a bouquet. Two months later she knew which flowers were cheaper, three months later she began to understand which vase is best for a particular bouquet, 4 months later she began experimenting with composition, 5 months later she was well versed in coloristics, 6 months later she did not arrive at our appointment without flowers. A year later, she admitted that it became a symbol of stability, and this experiment made her understand better than any book on self-development and became a starting point to say "no" to all the ugly things in her life. It became easy to give up something. You just compare it to the pleasure of a bouquet and the beauty of flowers.

Another important message is the pleasure of the process! After all, a bouquet is not a static thing, not a constant; it can change with the withering of its individual parts.

It is an interesting science to re-sort a bouquet and make a new one from the remaining bouquet. This is the birth of a new one.

If I still haven't convinced you to buy flowers, just wait. Although I don't think it's worth putting off living your life.

Notes

Collections and collecting: basic level

Collecting is a chance to add your own identity to any interior.

So, how to organize your collection or start collecting? You really like your collection, but no one notices it?

Perhaps it's the lack of a good place for it or the background. Collection should be multi-layered and organized. This greatly affects its perception. Small objects look good on elevations or at eye level.

I collect saltshakers and vintage tableware, so they stand on a specially designated shelf for everyone to see.

I also have a collection of hand-woven rugs and it is placed all over the house. My dream is to buy a wooden rack to change the rugs. I'll put it directly in the hallway.

Haven't started a collection yet? Here are some tips for beginners

Collection options:

- **Interior and coffee books**

    This collection option is suitable for everyone.

    A stack of such books can be a decoration for a coffee table, kitchen island and cabinets, for a hallway console, a bench, and even in the bathroom.

    In short, it is easy – just collect a theme that is close to your heart – be it travelling, design, landscaping, plants, art or photography.

- **Flower pots for plants**

    Another safe choice of the collection that has very practical use. Your house will quite literally blossom with its appearance.

- **Vintage tableware**

    Also extremely practical collection that can be used every day. Each table serving will turn into a fest and each reception – into an unforgettable evening.

- **Tablecloths and plate coasters**

    Again, thanks to their ability to add aesthetics to everyday life, I only welcome such collections.

- **Rugs**

    Rugs are unique items that can change an entire room at once. This is the easiest way to update the interior, add playfulness, color or "assemble" into a single ensemble. It's good to have a lot of tools for this.

- **Art**

    I'm sure that you can place countless paintings, posters and photos in every house. Therefore, collecting them is a noble deed.

- **Vases**

    The thing is, such a collection will help you master the habit of #flowersasabasicneed, and there are never too many of them. Beautiful unusual vases look great even without flowers. They can be placed on any horizontal surface in the house, and this will only add some coziness.

- **Collectible design**

    This is the most enjoyable kind of collection that deserves your attention. It's so nice to replace one chair at the kitchen table with Wassily Chair Bauhaus Edition by Marcel Breuer or replace the IKEA floor lamp with the Iconic Taccia Table Lamp by Flos. Replace the coffee maker with a Tom Dixon. It would be nice to see in each room a collectible that arouses curiosity, adds some history and doesn't make the room look like the visualizations of designers.

- **Trays**

    There are never too many trays in the house. They also serve well in the organization of storage, during serving and at the reception. That's why I find such a collection super useful.

Some examples of anti-collections:

- ✗ magnets
- ✗ plates on the wall. A few plates can decorate the interior, but the collection will make it look like a restaurant
- ✗ irons
- ✗ photo cameras – the same story as plates on the wall. It is hardly possible to decorate it beautifully in large quantities (I know a few men who would argue with this).
- ✗ items that already have entire museums dedicated to them
- ✗ oversized items (bicycles, sewing machines). They fit perfectly into the interior of the workshop, but are not suitable for home
- ✗ wine corks

COLLECTOR'S MANIFESTO:

- bring practical things from your travels that you will later use, but not the items just to put in the forefront. They can be coffee makers, plates, carpets. This way you will collect eclecticism at home in a natural way.
- if you do not have a collection, visit the flea market without planning to collect something: it is possible that this is where you will find a pretty thing for an unusual collection, which can become its beginning.
- before buying something, think about whether there is a similar thing in your collection.
- you do not necessarily need to be an avid collector, it is enough to be interested in the origin of the exhibits.
- collectibles can be incredibly prosaic: the main thing is to arrange them in groups
- think about what you liked as a child, or support your child's collection with more expensive exhibits – it's very interesting. Anime, posters, Disney figurines – that's just a small part of what you can collect together.
- do not admire very rare exhibits – the collection must be enriched from time to time, otherwise this "something" will remain the only vintage thing.
- do not buy one thing after another – choose only special things, so that each item in your collection will make you happy, and it will not just take up space.
- there is nothing wrong with buying an already assembled collection if you like it. You can always add items to it.

A FEW TIPS:

- in practice, when starting a collection, I would buy the first few items for it in one color, so it is easier to compose a small collection with few objects.
- if you do not know what to collect, you can collect not specific things but themes. You can't go wrong with thematic collections.
- for example, the Design Academy Eindhoven gives its graduates several topics for the final project within which they work, and when you see their works at the end, everything comes together, although the works are completely different. There are subject design, jewelry, household appliances, textiles, new technologies, and architecture. They are all united in a great way from the very beginning. Collecting should not be taken too seriously; it is a game and a process where at some point you will understand that you guessed right.
- do not confuse collecting with collectible design. Although design items, of course, can serve as the collection items. I mentioned them above.
- try to keep your trinkets localized. The whole apartment should not turn into a museum.

Most likely, you already have the beginning of the collection. Name three small items in the house. Find and use them to get started with your collection.

Art in your home: where to start?

Your home is sure to become the most resourceful place on your map once art pieces appear in it.

What exactly is art, you ask me?

If I had to describe it in one sentence, I would say: art is SOMETHING that touches your soul. Yes, the soul is a very abstract concept, an intangible sensation in the solar plexus or under our ribs. This is exactly what we feel every day when we hurt someone's feelings, when we kiss a child's head, when we help each other. Let people say that it's guilt, love, friendship – they are right. Because all these feelings live in our soul. That's the same "something" that you want to think about, that makes you think and that you want to return to mentally – that is art.

I want to share an allegory with you – about the grain of sand that became a pearl. Every time I am asked about the very first step in creating an inspiring home interior, I never get tired of talking about the starting point – about the piece of art that should be the first to settle in your house.

Here, it is important to look inside yourself, listen to your feelings, your thoughts and emotions. Choose not just "something interesting", but what you really like. Thus, you will trust the inner compass: confess to yourself your true desires. Specifically your own desires, and not imposed by someone. Imposition itself sometimes does not seem obvious, and it is not an act of violence. You just heard from everyone for a long time that something is beautiful, and you started to believe it. Therefore, at the moment of acknowledging your own taste, and to be precise from the moment you hang a picture or photo on the wall, which is felt with every fiber of your being – that's when a grain of sand appears, it gets into the shell and begins to turn into a pearl.

Not every grain of sand becomes a pearl. Yours will definitely not become one if you listen to other people's instructions, believe in other people's tastes or fool yourself. Suggestions and trends are your worst enemy.

It's never too late to begin! Even if you already have paintings, pictures, sculptures and other pieces of art in your house. Truly "your" item may appear at any time. It is your first piece of art that will begin to change everything around you: space, everyday life and the future.

In the interior, I like to combine modern art + classics + futurism. I came to this formula a long time ago, and my journey was long. I bought art pieces on the advice of art dealers, selected them based on color, "fell for" sales and made a lot of mistakes. I would not say it was bad – because I was buying experience. But if I had read this book, I would have stopped paying attention to everything but my own feelings about the object. I would not seek confirmation of its "beauty", status or investment. I would go back to Bordeaux and bought that little boy by an unknown author who was holding a paper plane. For me, the paper plane was a symbol of childhood, and I clearly remember my soul singing.

It's no secret that it is a matter of balance.

Simply putting a figurine / painting of a modern or other kind in the house is not about balance, it is about following the trends, perhaps, the desire to meet other people's expectations, the desire to astound, to challenge.

When it comes to art, many people first think of paintings. They are undoubtedly the most common form of art.

The following is a list of art pieces that can be your starting point:

- paintings
- posters
- pictures
- collages
- graphics
- illustrations
- object design – sofa, wardrobe, dressing table, mirrors, armchair, carpet, chair, table, vases, lamps
- ceramics, china
- wall art
- panel pictures
- sculptures
- embroidery
- batik
- textile (tablecloths, blankets, bedspreads, pillows).

Now is the time to think about "visual experience".

Observation is a very important, if not the only way to experience art in any form.

It is a well-known fact that when we stand, the neurons that trigger the process of walking are inactive. At the moment of silence, the neurons responsible for speech are "silent". When our neurons are not needed at some point, they are inactive. Our task is to turn on the neurons of contemplation of beauty more often and to do it consciously. Then the "sleeping neurons" will turn on and begin to develop important prospects and symbols for us, as well as determine the vector of our development for many years.

That is why it is important to take out all of the grandmother's dinner sets and use them daily; that is why, not for any other reason, you need to hang your own paintings and / or paintings of your favorite artists; that is why, being in a foreign city, it is worth spending money on the museum admission, where you will spend 30 minutes and after leaving you will no longer remember what you saw there; that is why you need to surround yourself with beautiful thoughts and buy flowers, that is why we should give each other emotions, not items.

If we go further, that is why it is worth taking children to music and drawing clubs, buying them unusual things and visiting secret cities and yards with them.

THE RULE:

If you want to see this piece of art in your house – then that is where it belongs. No advice or reflection.

Since this is a very practical book, I can't help but write about the role / tasks of art in the house:

- bring joy
- touch the soul
- tell meanings
- personify
- place accents
- motivate
- be nostalgic

All of these are not abstract, but quite specific examples of the role of art.

You will look through, come back to, and examine only what hooked you. The more multifaceted you are, the more things you are attracted to – that is why we have to collect everything in the house, from classics to futurism.

Another enemy of ours is the fear of ruining walls and renovations. Maybe it's too straightforward, but I think that 80% of the interior cannot be spoiled any further. They can only become better.

Finally, you will not believe it, but the holes in the walls can be fixed.

You renovate your house not for the walls. Walls and rooms serve you, and you are their full-fledged owner.

A trip to the flea market, what to focus on

Brocante, vintage fair, thrift shop, flea market, second-hand shop – these are the variety of a paradise for you while decorating your home.

My special list for the beginner of what you can buy there:

- flower vases for #flowersasabasicneed.
- trays – you can never have too many of them.
- candlesticks.
- lamp bases – with or without lampshade. And if you screw in Edison's light bulb, it will be very beautiful. Like floor lamps, it cannot be too many of bedside lamps.
- plates (single for solo serving and for serving in the style of "brocante").
- cachepots, flowerpots – copper, iron, porcelain.
- posters (floral or portraits), or sometimes even just framing from them.

If you're already on the "flea" and you did not manage to buy anything there, maybe you're just out of luck. Or maybe you didn't know the little secrets of successful purchases. There are four important points in this matter:

1. First, going to the flea market is a very energy-consuming process, even for well-trained haunters. It takes me only two hours to be completely exhausted, though I love it. A purchase made after these two hours is called "the greatest regret". Therefore, every minute is valuable.

2. Secondly, you may not have taken the time to prepare: wear comfortable shoes and simple clothes ("sophisticatedly" dressed customers sometimes pay twice as much). Determine a reasonable budget that you are ready to spend. Cash only.

3. Think of it as a fee for emotions and entertainment: as a trip to the movies or restaurants and as a new experience.

4. Take several large cotton bags or wheeled trolley with you – it will be much nicer. Lack of space is even worse than lack of budget: it ends faster than money.

SECRETS:

- Come to the flea market as early as possible, even before the opening. This is extremely important, because the same "hunters" buy the most valuable things very quickly.
- Have a small talk with the sellers, be friendly and do not forget to smile.
- Avoid stands with new items, but also avoid large collections. It is better to buy such things online.
- Prefer sellers who don't sell a ton of stuff.
- If you found one interesting item – look closely, perhaps, you will find a few more at the same seller!
- Remember that things in antique shops are more expensive, so if you buy "expensive" stuff here, it is a bargain anyway.
- Buy now. If you do not buy a thing right away, but have to get back to the item – it's a waste of time.
- Pay attention to the shape. You can change the color by repainting the item.
- Immediately think about where you will repair or restore preferred items. Contact the craftsmen, find out the price of the repair, and only then decide whether to buy the thing or not. Ideally, if you can take or send items immediately from the flea market to the repair shop. At home, when the euphoria subsides after buying an item, such things turn into ordinary clutter.
- Do not consider the functionality of the thing you liked. It's not about that, it's about emotions.

Canonical design items

The task of this chapter is to inspire you to buy at least one thing from the series of subject design.

Such things are often very distinctive and emotional. They "talk" in the interior with the residents of the house, with guests-experts in design, and in a completely inconspicuous way hypnotize those who are not yet familiar with them.

In this chapter, I want to introduce you to the bright stars of subject design. These timeless interior items do not become obsolete over the years, but on the contrary, like cognac or wine, acquire additional value and chic.

Subject or industrial design appeared in England in the 18th century, when not only how the object looks became important, but also how it will be technically executed and how easy it is to launch into mass production. It was the most important issue in the era of the industrial revolution. This is how the profession of a designer came into existence – a person who devised the appearance of a product and how it will be arranged from a technical point of view.

At the same time, so-called behavioral design emerged – a design that influences people's behavior. Thus, the supermarket cart (created in 1937 by Sylvan Goldman, owner of the American shops Standard Grocery and Humpty Dumpty) encourages people to buy more and thus changes behavioral habits. Likewise, large refrigerators and even a toothbrush, which made morning and evening hygienic procedures a habit, affected people.

Many items went down in history due to their extremely convenient design, many have managed to change everyday life, some have changed the culture of consumption, created entire professions, and some have changed the world.

I have two arguments as to why you should pay attention to them:

1. They do not go down in price. Buying a designer item can be considered an investment, sometimes more successful, sometimes less – but by buying this thing, you can definitely sell it no cheaper than you bought it. Why? The thing is that people do not part with such things by their will, they are quite expensive, and sometimes they are not so easy to find. Sometimes they are made in limited edition, and then the thing becomes a real rarity. There are millions of books on subject design, and they are all about the task of finding the same story related to one of these subjects that will make you want to buy it.

2. Such things fit into any interior; they nurture your taste and the taste of the inhabitants of your home for a long time. They are very expressive. You can make an experiment and rent such a thing or borrow from someone for a while. In a month of "cohabitation", you will understand why canonical things are called that. They are like tattoos: once you've done one, it's hard for you to stop. There are very few of them here, because the book is about something else. But they will definitely inspire you to explore the world of design.

I will not number them, because the numbers can turn my list into a ranking, but in fact they are all the best of the best, and who will take the lead on the pedestal of design in your heart, only you can decide.

Wassily armchair 1925

I will start with one of my favorites – Wassily armchairs by Hungarian designer Marcel Breuer. At first sight, I immediately imagined it in my house.

The author's chair was inspired by the handlebars of his own bicycle. The value of "Wassily" design is the bold idea of using steel tubes as elements of the furniture frame. Leather or fabric is stretched between the steel tubes, creating a hammock effect. Sitting in it feels like floating in the air.

It is said that Vasyl Kandynskyi, passing by Breuer's office when he was assembling the chair, was shocked and asked to do the same for him. To which Breuer replied, "Of course I will, Vasyl!"

Lamps PH Henningsen (by Danish designer Paul Henningsen) – the first specialist in the field of lighting. This revolutionary as for that time, multi-level shading system, which gives the light a golden glow, is the most beautiful indirect light that "reflects".

The story of these lamps is the story of family ties and the desire to help his mother. At that time there was not enough variety of lamps (she was born in 1868 and lived to be 93 years old), but the designer's mother clearly understood that lighting could affect the external beauty: with one light, you look good, with another – not really. Agnes Katinka Malling Henningsen was a writer and activist for the sexual freedom movement. Of course, she was often dissatisfied with the bright light of modern light bulbs, because the overhead lighting highlighted all the wrinkles on her face. The key feature of Henningsen lamps is their aesthetics: even when the light is off, the lamp is perceived as an art object. It is almost impossible to forge them due to the complexity of the design, and PH Artichoke is my favorite design icon of the 20th century.

Now let's move on to the Finns.

Stool 60 Alvara Aalto, 1930 – the most famous stool in the world

The reasons for this are the availability of material and ease of production, and hence the low price and potential for mass sales. In all official Apple showrooms, you can see Stool 60 by Finnish architect Alvar Hugo Aalto.

This is the first in the world piece of furniture made of bent glued plywood. A special feature of the chair was a smoothly curved leg at an angle of 90 degrees. Aalto came up with such a leg while looking at his skis (and you know what skis are for a boy in a Finnish forest!). The key feature of this three-legged friend is that the chairs can be easily kept one on top of another, creating an object of art, a real sculpture, similar to human DNA. That is, the architect, creating it, thought not only about the chair itself, but also about how it will look in the assembled form. For me this is an indicator of mastery. The Japanese also don't only think about the architectural structure, but about how this structure will be destroyed as well. That is where they start.

Who do you think is the most famous copyist of the most famous Finnish chair? This is the Swedish company IKEA, which has been selling its version for over a decade – the "Frosta" stool. Thank you at least for the price (about 10 euros), because the original costs about 200 euros.

Juicy Salif juicer by Philip Stark, 1990

We move on to the world's most famous juicer Juicy Salif by guru of modern design Philip Stark. In practice, it is, of course, more of an art object than a juicer, but it has not become less popular and desirable. This brilliant idea came to the artist during a trip to Italy, in a restaurant over a plate of fresh squid. Inspired, Stark immediately sketched the future product on a napkin with ketchup.

I always ask you to act. The action must take place right after the idea; otherwise, the idea loses its meaning – so Stark immediately sent a sketch to Alberto Alessi, owner of the famous Italian company Alessi. In 1990, a new product appeared in stores.

Its unique space design couldn't be confused with anything, it was truly a cult thing.

Philip Stark's juicer serves a more exotic than functional purpose. This object changed the whole philosophy of design, which is set out in the book "Emotional Design" by Donald Norman: form must correspond to emotions, not functions.

Dalù table lamp and Carimate chair by Vico Magistretti

"To achieve simplicity – is the most difficult thing in design," "Design looks at household items with eyes full of curiosity." These quotations are the leitmotif not only of the work of Vico Magistretti, an Italian designer and architect (1920-2006), but probably partly of mine. Just think about it, because all these canonical objects are very simple, they do not have extra ornaments. It is this simplicity that gives them character and timeless actuality. His simple Carimate chair, designed for the Carimate Golf Club, became a cult designer item in the 60's. The chair was a duo of natural materials – wood and reeds – and bright modern work with paint and lacquer coating. Carimate became a symbol of London culture and the Beatles.

The Dalù lamp was originally available in black and white, it was quite affordable and in demand. Its last edition was in 2005: without changing the original form, more bright colors were added to the line – for color connoisseurs like me.

The Egg armchair from the guru of Scandinavian minimalism Arne Jacobsen in 1958

For fifty years, the Egg armchair has rightfully held the title of a bright representative of the iconic Scandinavian style in furniture design.

It has an egg shape and a rather concise design. Simplicity of lines that follow the body contours and provide comfort, a bright palette of colors and high quality materials – that's the secret of the success of this chair. Half a century after its creation, this iconic design object will be called a classic of furniture art.

The iconic dsw Eames chair by American designers Charles and Ray Eames

The thing you undoubtedly have seen, or perhaps even have in your kitchen or office, but you don't even know its history. This chair is still considered to be the most comfortable chair in history due to its pressure relief across the waist.

Eames became the first plastic chair to go into mass production, and right away – it became a world wide hit: now designer furniture has become available, including for the middle class.

They have a wide range of combinations – backings, seats and colors, so they are constantly used in cafes and restaurants, home offices, living rooms and kitchens, conference rooms and outdoor terraces. This design is, of course, copied by anyone who wants to (while the rights to make furniture from designers Charles and Ray Eames belong to two world manufacturers: Herman Miller and Vitra). Thus, the impression of it is similar to the impression of a track that you like and that you have listened to too many times. For me, this is an example of folk design, and of course, I would put only the original chair – and in 50 years.

You will certainly be interested to explore:

- cast chairs by Werner Panton
- Eames Lounge Chair, which wherever it appears, gives the interior charm and "expensiveness"
- floor lamp Arco Achilles and Pierre Giacomo Castiglioni
- table lamp Original 1227 by George Carvardin, which became the prototype of a cute lamp on the official Pixar intro…

These design objects are real pieces of art that have gone down in history. They are admiring and inspiring, copied and sought after.

All items from this chapter are great examples of iconic design. The real power of design is change of life, not commercial success. But as always, if you love what you do, it will definitely be commercially successful.

We are surrounded by products that significantly change everyday life – from a toothbrush to a mixer, from airbags to trolleys in the supermarket. Design is like air – if all goes well, we don't notice it, but as soon as something goes wrong, we suffocate.

The whole selection is not only canonical, it is a responsible design, because only by combining high-quality materials and inspiration, you can create irreplaceable things, not disposable things.

In general, immersing yourself in the topic of canonical design objects is very, very interesting! Firstly, it develops your awareness no worse than exhibitions, and secondly, it's great stories, because each subject is a novel, a detective story, and sometimes comedy. Third, every story is a business school case, it is learning in its purest form – marketing, innovation and approach.

Notes

#GeorgeCabinet, or start your relationship with retro items

You will tell me you do not like retro. And I'll say that you don't know how to handle it.

There is no one who will not keep the cute little thing of his/her grandmother/great-grandmother and will not protect it from descendants, ironically purchased for them.

I also received scales and many other discordant things that may not be useful, but they warm the cockles of my heart, so I can hardly get rid of them.

But how to fit them into the interior? Such things go well with modern ones, because they are fed by contrast.

There are a few important points you need to know about retro.

- Retro is a history. This means that you need to know it, come up or tell the story of purchase, motivation. This should be done for children, family and friends.
- If there are other modern works and ceramics in the interior, then paintings and old posters are a safe choice in such situation.
- Use a maximum of 2 retro things in one space or create compositions with them (which can include up to 5-6 small different things).
- Any preserved thing may not be used for their intended purpose, but put them in a frame and hang them on a wall or put them in acrylic.
- Use Corten steel and make gallery captions for old paintings or modern ways of hanging and lighting.
- Make them part of history. Good photographers say that photos are successful, if you can look at a photo and come up with your own story or script. If old things can tell a story, it is worth continuing it with new things.
- Use antiques for other purposes, for example: stove as a plant stand, scales as a sugar bowl, chair as a bedside table, etc.
- Eclecticism is about care. Retro things require more care and attention.
- Retro is antiques and vintage, don't confuse them with things that were in use. There is also a rarity – these are rare things made in limited quantities. It can be a modern object, and the value is in its uniqueness. Antiques are antiquarian things that are over

50 years old and have historical and artistic value. In the United States, antiques are items made before 1830, in Canada – before 1847. Vintage is younger things, about 15-50 years old, but with obvious signs of fashion of its time.

Don't have anything of retro? Go to the nearest flea market or print a photo from your childhood, find an old sweater, embroidery, a toy, advertisement or poster, photos of the times when you were a teenager, and do not be afraid to experiment.

Each thing is not exactly a thing, it is a dance, a story, exactly in the form in which you tell it to children, friends and neighbors, and to yourself. Remember, every purchased thing can become retro. Would you like your children to keep it?

Inspiration for change in your home and where to look for it

Inspiration is a very specific feeling. It makes the "wings appear," it makes the "butterflies flutter in your stomach," almost as because of love, your heart beats faster and eyes shine happily. There is an easy way to check if you are inspired: if you are ready to get up early in the morning and do it during the day.

Inspiration is definitely not something to remember when you are already fed up with the objects around you, furniture and walls. Willpower and a psychologist would help here. You should also mention inspiration only when you are suddenly overwhelmed by a creative crisis.

Inspiration won't just come of its own accord, it's a vaccine against depression and boredom.

Sitting and waiting for the muse to finally come to you makes absolutely no sense, so you can become an epic "snorp". Creative processes, like all others, are organization and rigid time management. This is how this book was written, otherwise you, my readers, would have been waiting for it for years.

Inspiration is a way of life. It keeps us in shape, allows us to do good deeds, get insights and work for pleasure.

What I suggest: Explore the mechanisms of inspiration.

Such mechanisms are:

1. Think.
2. Organize and plan.
3. Implement into or create an ecosystem.

1. THINK

Me, myself and I in every context. There is one constant in all manifestations of inspiration – it is you. Only what you pay attention to develops. I can't stand general words! What is inspiration? It's everywhere, well, damn, that's how it is! I tend to call inspiration a habit that is easy to develop, as well as the habit of seeing opportunities. The habit of being inspired comes when you:

- inspire someone else
- notice the beauty in the little things
- live here and now
- celebrate positive moments in your life
- make action plans in a state of inspiration.

Inspiration is an energy drink for an Ironman triathlete.

But first there was a dream, then training and an action plan.

When you lose inspiration, you can still move on inertia for a while, but it is also important to recharge in time. Eventually, this state is quite easy to enter. I'm used to collecting inspiration, and it's not running out, because it's honestly laid out on the shelves in the treasury of memories, like in the cartoon "Inside Out".

Just don't think that I suggest you "flutter in empirics and spray nectar of happiness." Sometimes you have to live your negative state. But man is born to be happy – and to become such is the direct task of life.

To inspire you, I want to encourage you to think.

To begin with, consider what you have (or own) that no one else has? What are your strengths? What overwhelms you? Maybe you have a large, rich library, grandmother's recipes, an old notebook with the phones of a seamstress and a family moneylender?

Maybe you take unsurpassed black and white photos. Maybe you love India and Istanbul at the same time. Do you admire of taxas to the insanity, do you cry from French cinema? What does the interior say about it?

2. ORGANIZE AND PLAN

Where do I find inspiration for constant change in my home?

PINTEREST

A great resource for inspiration, but here the main thing to remember is that the enemy of inspiration is clutter.

Lots of folders, incomprehensible screenshots, heaps of cluttered information and a variety of photos without a clear plan of action. Inspiration = plan. Success = order.

Therefore, when you collect ideas, immediately create folders and sign "accomplish by December 2020", "make by March 2021"… and constantly review them and delete what is no longer relevant.

CINEMA

Its incredible advantage is that it can be combined with brushing up your English and watch movies in the original with subtitles. English is a must, I'm serious.

🎞 TV Series:

- The world's most extraordinary homes
- Designs
- Tiny house nation
- Amazing interiors
- Stay here
- The great interior design challenge
- Grand
- Downton Abbey
- Bridgerton

🎥 Movies:

- Portrait of a Beauty (2008)
- A Good year
- Youth (2015, Paolo Sorrentino)
- Outbreak (1995)
- Last year in Marienbad (1961, Alain Rene)
- The Age of Innocence (1983, Martin Scorsese)
- I am Love (Luca Guadagnino)
- The Big Bang Theory (Luca Guadagnino)
- Call me by your name (Luca Guadagnino)
- The Remains of the Day (1993, James Ivory)
- Orlando
- Garden
- Only Lovers Left Alive
- Piano
- The Draughtsman's Contract (1982 Peter Greenway)
- Gattaca
- F for Fake (1973, Orson Welles)
- Loving Vincent (2017)
- Exit through the Gift Shop (2010, Banksy)

- My Masterpiece (2018)
- French Dispatch (2020, Wes Anderson)
- The Dreamers (2003)
- Stealing Beauty (1996)
- Marie Antoinette (2005)
- La Dolce Vita (1960, Federico Fellini)
- The Lovers (2012)

 **Books:**

- Vincent Darre: Surreal Interiors of Paris
- Rebecca Atwood "Living in Color"
- Rebecca Atwood "Life with Ornament"
- Donald Norman "Emotional Design"
- All ASSOULINE Books
- TACHEN Books

Other:

- Adweek.com
- Adage.com
- R / GA
- Bredyatkin Podcast
- BOOKSTORES: How to Read More Books in the Golden Age of Content

3. COMMUNICATION

Nothing is as inspiring as people and their stories. Small talk is a wonderful thing. An interesting story happened to me during "Three days of design" in Stockholm.

The group and I arrived at the next location – Muuto design. The house was old, the elevator was designed for a small number of people, and I stayed downstairs. Some people went to the elevator, some decided to go up on foot.

While I was waiting for the elevator, I joked with a stranger who was also waiting for the elevator. Probably, the inability to take pauses or the habit of small talks spoke to me. I don't remember what the joke was, but he said he worked in this building. I complimented him on the place of work, and what was my surprise, when it turned out that he was the owner of Muuto. It became immediately clear when he got out of the elevator.

Is it fair to say that we had a wonderful tour, even in those rooms where visitors are usually not allowed?

4. MENTORSHIP, INSPIRATION FROM FAMOUS AND SUCCESSFUL PEOPLE

"The best thing about a head of state is the opportunity to talk on the phone with anyone in the world," said Barack Obama. In this sense, each of us is a president. The modern world allows everyone to use this option. You can tweet Mask, write on Oprah's FB or comment on Philip Stark, argue in the comments with…. After all, as Yuval Noah Harari summed up, the very desire to communicate is one of the most powerful forces driving a person. "Homo sapiens conquered the world because he possessed such an instrument as speech."

5. MUSEUMS, EXHIBITIONS, PRESENTATIONS

But it's not them that matter, it's the people you go there with (because there's nothing accidental!), especially if you haven't known them before (such design tours are a great option for those who do not know English, or for those who do not want to travel alone). And the people who are waiting for you there as the host. Such trips are quite successfully organized by Larisa Tsybina and Creascope.

Visiting exhibitions is important for you not because of trends and a variety of ideas – it is also in Pinterest. This is important for the sake of the living people there who are capable of the biggest challenge in life.

The atmosphere itself is conducive and intoxicating, so it's a sin not to take advantage of it!

The list of exhibitions is below; just choose one of them to visit, and the influx of endorphins is guaranteed. Their dates change every year, but the essence remains:

- AMBIENTE, Frankfurt – Large range of products on the themes of HoReCa.
- NOMAD CIRCLE, St. Moritz – Created in 2016, a mobile exhibition of collectible design and contemporary art.
- CLERKENWELL DESIGN WEEK, London. Clerkenwell is one of the largest art clusters in the world. It used to have factories and plants, but now houses artists, designers and architects from all over the district.
- HEIMTEXTIL, Frankfurt. On Heimtextil it makes sense to go to connoisseurs of fabrics and upholstery, wallpaper, bedding and kitchen linen, carpets, but most importantly – not trends, but technology.
- CES – CONSUMER ELECTRONICS SHOW, Las Vegas. The world's most prestigious platform for consumer electronics and electrical appliances that determine the future.
- IMM COLOGNE, Cologne – a large furniture fair.
- MAISON & OBJET / Paris – the largest exhibition of everything in the world, including products from Ukrainian manufacturers.
- TORONTO DESIGN OFFSITE FESTIVAL (DESIGNTO) Toronto – Design event with more than a hundred exhibitions and events.
- CEVISAMA, Valencia – International Ceramics Exhibition.
- STOCKHOLM FURNITURE & LIGHT FAIR, Stockholm – Leading events for Scandinavian design.
- MODERNISM WEEK, Palm Springs and the most important architecture Mid-century modern.
- DESIGN INDABA, Cape Town – Every year the festival presents an interesting program consisting of performances by African musicians, filmmakers, designers and restaurateurs.
- TEFAF, Maastricht – Fair, one of the leading in the field of inventive art, antiques and design.
- DESIGN SHANGHAI, Shanghai – Just an incredible action on the other side of the planet. DesignTalks with famous local and international designers.
- MELBOURNE DESIGN WEEK, Melbourne – Australia's premier festival – a platform for communication, negotiation and exchange of experiences of all representatives of the design industry.

- DESIGN MARCH, Reykjavik – Local exhibition with workshops on architecture and fashion, graphic and promdesign.
- DRAWING NOW, Paris – Salon of modern drawing, will be interesting to decorators and interior stylists.
- PAD PARIS, Paris – Exhibition dedicated to furniture, jewelry, art and antiques, extremely popular among decorators for the uniqueness of the exhibits.
- SALONE DEL MOBILE MILANO, Milan – Important design exhibition in Europe.
- MILAN DESIGN WEEK, Milan – Milan Design Week goes hand in hand with the furniture salon and goes beyond the exhibition complex into the city.
- FRIEZE NEW YORK, New York – Innovative and experimental, new works: demonstration products mustn't be older than a year.
- VENICE ARCHITECTURAL BIENNALE, Venice – Main event of Italy, with quality training and worldwide popularity.
- ART BASEL, Basel – Annual Arts Fair. Here are the best galleries from around the world, including Gagosian, Thaddaeus Ropac, Lisson, White Cube, David Zwirner.
- MASTERPIECE LONDON, London – One of the leading exhibitions for cross-collectors. The best inventions of art, design, furniture and jewelry from antiquity to the present day.

Exhibitions come and go: Singapore, Milan, Paris, Eindhoven... Do not blame yourself if you did not get to visit all of them. The Internet will help you to follow the trends – just enter the exhibition you are interested in on Google or social networks and follow the geolocation. You get all the information first hand. It is impossible to visit all the exhibitions, as it is not possible to be aware of all the events. But if you know briefly and clearly about the most important things that are happening around you – it speaks of you as an interesting interlocutor.

Let's call it "what runs this week": always know what drives this week.

6. IMPLEMENT INTO OR CREATE AN ECOSYSTEM

In an ideal world, I would create an ecosystem from my way of life. So that its space entered the lives of my loved ones. I would like them to learn to do cool things from me, learn new information, try to spend more time in my space, turn it into a part of their daily lives.

The main idea of the ecosystem is the relationship. Thanks to it, the elements of the ecosystem are growing. Each part of it increases the chances of survival through communication with another ecosystem. At the same time, the possibility of ecosystem survival increases with the number of integrated / associated living organisms.

Integration is an important word. That's why English is so important.

Ecosystems also offer ways to build them (Design living / kaizen) and other ways to effectively manage and make a difference (PR and personal brand).

To keep fit and constantly on the wave, I offer to make a plan-grid of self-inspiration, building your ecosystem and working on ways to effectively manage it: personal brand and PR.

I also advise you to work on increasing social ties and pay attention to increasing the number of organisms associated with it.

Look at the exhibition dates a year ahead. Maybe one of them will even coincide with your vacation in another country, you will combine a pleasant thing with a useful one.

Schedule movie watching. It's ridiculous to hope that someone will ask you or remind you to watch a movie. If we even have a need to plan having sex in this fleeting world, what about inspiration then? So, we can at least be sure that we will have time to watch the movie.

Turn your home into a place that welcomes and inspires you.

There is nothing more permanent than temporary.

And finally, I may surprise you, but in my home there are:

100% love and self-acceptance.
95% of furniture is moved and carried.
90% of the decorations were bought on trips.
85% of furniture is not new (reuse, reduce or recycle).
80% of my interior I am satisfied with.

75% of my collections – spontaneous purchases.
70% of my purchases stay with me for no more than a year.
65% of colored decor and furniture elements.
60% of the furniture I made over and use for other purposes.
55% I bought for resale, without a specific purpose.
50% of my house belongs to my husband.
45% of paintings are the works of young artists.
40% will be inherited by my children.
35% of my purchases – subject design.
30% left from previous owners without improvement and change.
25% compromises with loved ones.
20% of art – photos.
15% of children's art.
10% of my house is given to my guests.
5% of my house was given to me.
0% of my house is left unattended.

I would like to go back to the beginning and remind you that what you are paying attention to is developing.

Notes

Home hacks: unobvious things

You may find the information in this chapter funny. The futurists were also laughed at. In general, this whole book is a continuous life hack. All life hacks I've tested and they justify their value.

1. Dishwashers. If there are more than three family members, it will definitely not be money wasted! Children and their friends, your guests and relatives will be happy when the process of washing dishes is fully delegated to machinery. It can also be a place to store dishes, because on an ordinary day it is convenient to take clean dishes from one niche, and to put dirty dishes in another.

2. Shelves in the kitchen plinth. Even if you have a very large kitchen, there is always something to put there! With such a place for storage, you may not make the top drawers for storage in the kitchen, and if you do it, only to the ceiling, so that there is no place for dust.

3. A cool pantry near the kitchen is a combination of a large refrigerator with a large cupboard, which can store both food and canning and juices, and most importantly – a mixer, steamer, multicooker and food processor: assembled and ready at any moment to be used.

4. Empty shelf. I would even single out two of such shelves, if it is possible. Really, it's a cool thing. The whole chapter is devoted to it.

5. Buy vases for different flowers: at least 5 different in size and material. To place #flowersasabasicneed in them in any season prettily. Volumetric vase – for peonies, lilacs; assorted – for bouquets; high – for roses, sunflowers; rose bowl – for slices, and a vase for one flower.

6. Wreath hanger. This is exactly what we need when the New Year comes, and you do not know how to attach such a beautiful new Christmas wreath.

7. Turn off the lights in the house with one switcher. Such a great switcher, when lazy to run back, is right at the exit. It will be especially appreciated by owners of multi-level / storied houses and apartments.

8. Heated floor at the entrance. In winter, it dries shoes and immediately warms up nicely.

9. Two washing machines. If it is possible and there is some space, then it greatly simplifies life. Clothes for babies and allergy sufferers or just jeans after a walk with your favorite dog can be washed immediately without risk to the clothes of other residents.

10. Hook on the back of a high chair. It is very convenient if the bib is always at hand.

11. If you are the lucky owner of a house with 2 floors and more, then provide **storage space for a mop and all other accessories on each floor.** This is very convenient and facilitates the cleaning process.

12. Socket inside the bathroom cabinet. It is convenient to plug in an electric toothbrush, razor or hair dryer and not remove the cord from the socket every time.

13. Create a family logo once for all. This is a great birthday gift and will continue to help personalize the space: logo rugs in front of the door, glasses and appliances with initials, napkins and tablecloths. You can order a logo from a graphic designer.

14. Ice bucket with mascarons. This is the most universal thing I've ever seen. It can be used at least in 40 ways; it always creates a mood and attracts attention.

15. Hammock in the bath for wet toys. That is how sailors dried their clothes, and it will make life easier for those of us who have children.

16. Hang a wreath of herbs or a bouquet of dried flowers directly above the cane in the shower. The aroma "as after rain" is provided.

17. If you want to update the door – **paint the ends and canvas in different colors.**

18. Scented sachets in cabinets with clothes and bedding, scented candles in the compartment for dishes are the best investments.

19. An ostrich feather duster will turn cleaning decor items into a pleasant ritual.

20. IKEA magnetic knife holders can be used in the children's room for wall storage of small metal cars.

The purpose of this chapter is to teach you to see such "life hacks" anywhere: in a hotel, in a rented apartment, on vacation, at friends', on Pinterest, to keep such a list and implement it.

Comfort is not created by expensive things, but by the proper investment in comfort.

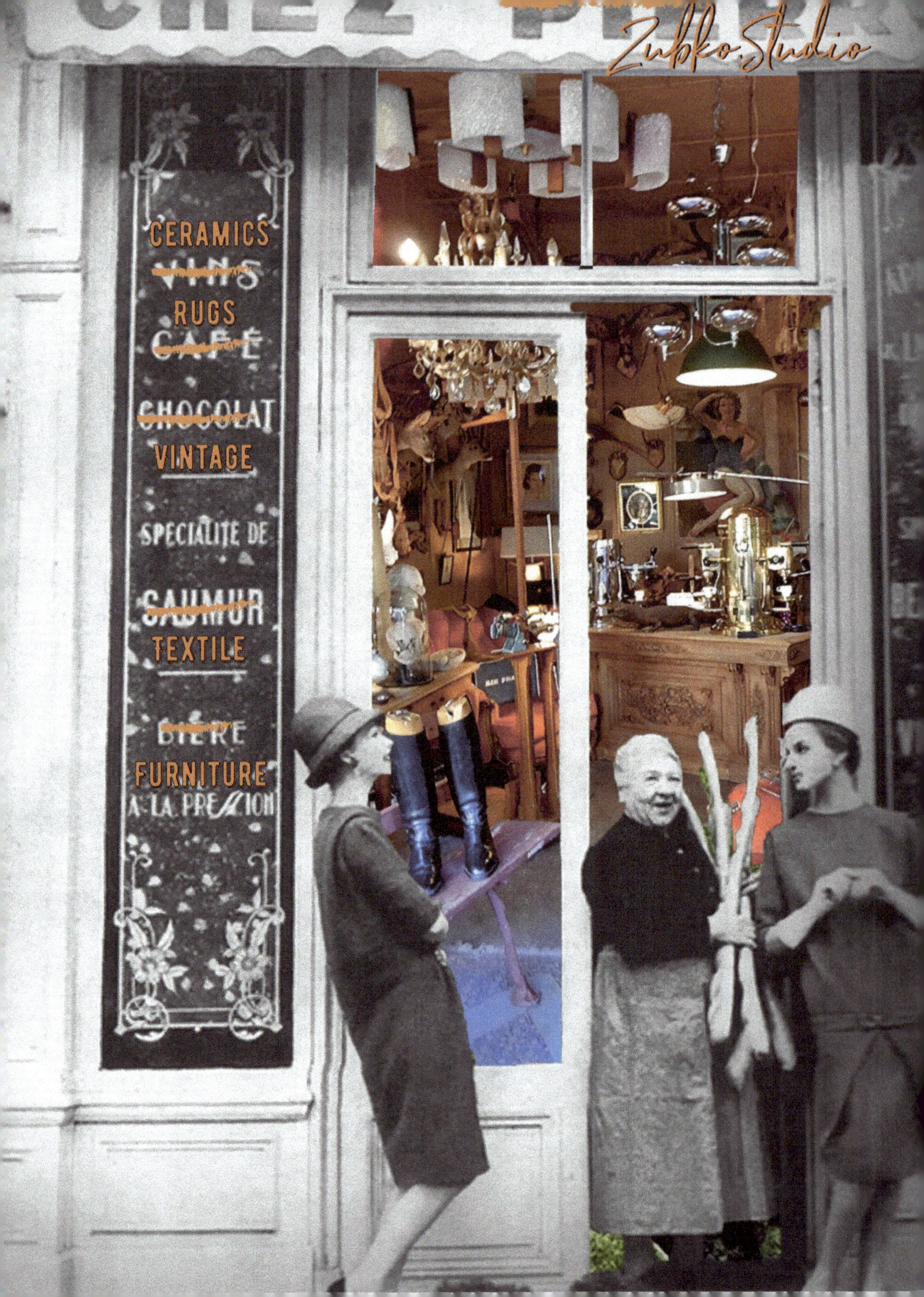
Zubko.Studio
CERAMICS
VINS
RUGS
CAFÉ
CHOCOLAT
VINTAGE
SPECIALITE DE
SAUMUR
TEXTILE
BIERE
FURNITURE
A LA PRESSION

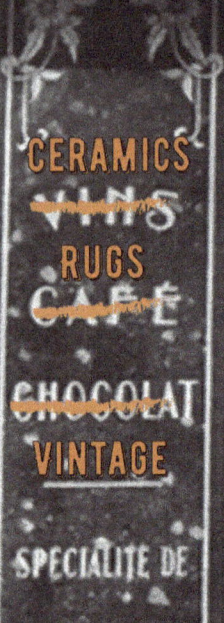

Where to do the shopping?

I keep nothing a secret and always share my findings, favorite brands and cool masters on Instagram if possible.

I receive personal messages and e-mails almost every day with the questions "Where to buy? Is it better here or there? How much does it cost?". But I am especially fascinated by the fact that these people "feeling the wind of change, do not build a wind shield, but a windmill." I will be happy to help them with this.

Since I have been observing the development of the Ukrainian interior products market for more than a year, I can say that the number and quality of Ukrainian manufacturers, stores with a good selection of decor, showrooms and vintage suppliers have grown significantly and continues to grow.

How do I choose brands? I like the quote from the movie "The Social Dilemma": "If you're not paying for the product, you are the product." This film is based on a dialogue with former employees of Facebook, Google, Instagram, the main insight of which is that our behavior is controlled not for our benefit, but for the benefit of sellers and advertisers, who encourage us to consume more. At one time, the invention of the two-compartment refrigerator had a significant impact on the market for food, and the advent of the freezer has lifted the entire Australian economy.

Now, in a time of rapid development of production and innovation, I acutely feel that all brands in the world are not covered, and is it necessary at all?

I have a few principles according to which I buy decorations. They can be used when buying goods in any industry.

1. I have confidence in the person behind the brand of the store, what is her\his name and what are their values in life? I would rather leave the money for Anna at a coffee shop around the corner so she can pay for aikido for her son than for a stranger from McDonald's.

2. How employees feel about their work, whether they are brand advocates. People often like their work when it is valued by management, and this "charges" the product with positive energy. Everyone is satisfied – both the one who produces the product and the one who buys it.

3. Flexibility of the company: whether it is ready for unusual situations, whether it responds sincerely to requests, or reluctantly formally.

4. Openness and sense of humor. How employees of the company behave offline and online: whether they respond quickly (and whether they respond at all), how they perceive criticism and suggestions. In Japan, when you write a letter to an employee who is not in charge of your question, he always sends it to a specialist who can help, while in Europe 30-40% of the company's employees do not respond to such letters at all.

5. Intimacy and involvement. This is about activities, community building and customer involvement in the customer-employee-service relationship. This means that you are always offered a little more than you expect.

6. Service and the ability to keep small talk. It is an illusion that work for us is just work. We live it every day, and it is important that we are surrounded by nice people at work. Small talk is an indicator of a decent level of brand service, it is mandatory.

7. Transparent algorithm of interaction with the manufacturer (measurements, discounts). It should be added that real money for brands is brought by ordinary customers, not bloggers. That's why it's so important to treat each of your clients as a millionaire blogger.

8. Clear margins. We are ready to pay more when we understand what we are overpaying for, and we are not ready – when the

monopolist, selling his product, makes a big markup, without confirming it with anything. The market dictates the conditions. We must not compromise.

Below I have tried to gather those brands that meet these principles. So here is a list of brands that I often buy for myself and for my customers, and the products, and their quality are pleasantly impressive. You have already met many in the book, but for the convenience of searching, if you need a particular type of decoration, I divided the list into categories and tried to gather everything here. If you have a desire to bring something interesting from vacation or you decide to expand the geographical boundaries of the decor, I have also added world manufacturers.

CERAMICS:

"Yedyna – exclusive ceramics"
yedinaceramics
yedinaceramics
Handmade home lamps and décor. Ceramic lamps of the most unusual shapes have become a wonderful discovery for me.

The Art Room Ceramics
www.theartroomceramics.com
the.art.room.ceramics
Very cool ceramic dishes for the table serving. Cups, saucers of extraordinary shapes. But its discovery for me was super cool thing – ceramic noses for sunglasses and a key box.

Chamotte ceramics
e.demerdzhy.ceramics

Here you can be find some more beautiful ceramics:
- Rezon
- Gorn
- Hmarunka
- Quiet form
- Gumenchuk

- Maistrenko ceramics
- Ceramic art studio "Kust"
- Sofika
- Pretty plate
- Ceramicforhomeandsoul
- Naturaceramica
- Dotork ceramics

RUGS:

PupchaKilim
◉ pupcha_kilim

I'll just say that all the carpets in my house are from PupchaKilim! She is incredibly talented and soon every carpet will be especially valuable, as she only sells a single copy of each.

Lorena Canals
⌂ www.rugs.in.ua
◉ rugs.in.ua

Spanish brand of cotton rugs No1 Lorena Canals for children's rooms, bedrooms, kitchens, terraces and other rooms in the house. Woolable by Lorena Canals are the world's first wool carpets, which can be washed.

You can find some more beautiful rugs here:
- Gushka.wool
- Zvyazani
- Oleziolezi
- Oksana Levchenya
- Ivanka carpet
- KilimArt studio

BEDDING:

La Perla Home Ukraine
⌂ www.laperlahomeukraine.com
◉ laperla_home_ukraine

Famous Italian quiet luxury. Yes, it's expensive. But to feel like Queen, relaxing on such a set, it's worth it!

You can find some more beautiful bedding here:
- Laurel Home
- Devoe Home
- Home Me
- Leglo
- Postelka
- Airy Li store
- Shana Home

FURNITURE AND HOME ACCESSORIES:

Laurel Home
www.laurelhome.com.ua
laurel_home
Design bureau with a cozy showroom in the city center and its own manufacturing. Custom-made furniture made of natural oak massif. In addition to furniture, in Laurel Home you will find a great choice décor – candles, linen bedding and tableware.

Drommel
www.drommel.com.ua
drommel.furniture
drommel_furniture
Furniture without unnecessary filter, which helps to focus on the main thing. The brand simplifies the process of choosing and buying furniture, offering ready-made solutions for arranging space. With competent and good service, individual orders are taken in the direction of Drommel Select.

Decor2art
decor2art
I am in love with their tables and bedside tables. They boldly and very successfully experiment with shape, material and color. I love the brave.

Drevych
🏠 www.drevych.ua
f drevych_ua
⊙ drevych_ua

Artisan family production of furniture and décor for walls made of wood. Here they work with the preservation of Ukrainian carpentry techniques, making exclusive wooden furniture, wall décor and panel paintings, and even wooden mosaics.

Some more beautiful furniture can be found here:
- FILD
- Woodwerk
- Solovero
- Crafter
- Woo Furniture
- HIS
- Buro150

VINTAGE:

barhat home
⊙ Barhat.home
Here you will find vintage from different parts of the world and eras. Barhat home – one of the best suppliers of wheeled tables. I have often been asked about the chair on the cover of this book, so here it is, also from them!

Shabby store
⊙ shabby.store
f shabby.store.ua
This store has a good selection of vintage dishes and cutlery. I also advise you to look at the vintage trays – they are universal.

Golden Garbuz
🏠 www.auctionsline.com
⊙ yellow_garbuz_gallery
A unique account from the auction house that has been operating since 1997: both offline and online.

Vintage antique kiev
⊙ vintage.antique.kiev

Marmur studio
🅞 marmur.studio
Good selection of goods. Vlada has good taste and smell :) If you like how this book smells, thank Vlada.

Avrora Batyreva
🅞 avrorabatyreva
Vintage buyer.

You can have a closer look at vintage here:
- Korzina club
- Buro.vintage
- Chudodikovina
- Snail_s_house
- Mitskevich_co

HOME SCENTS:

MAISON BERGER PARIS
🏠 www.maisonbergerparis.com
🅞 maisonbergerparisua
Lamps of incredible beauty that not only aromatize air in the room, but also clean it. Today Maison Berger Paris offers a wide variety of models of lamps and fragrances, and the most important thing is the clean air in your home. It is noteworthy that Bergé lamps eliminate unpleasant odors at the molecular level.

Poetry Home
🏠 www.poetryhome.com
🅕 poetryhome.ua
🅞 poetry.home

WOOD MOOD candles
🏠 www.mywoodmood.com
🅞 mywoodmood
A family team that came up with the idea to combine a candle and a fireplace – and create the interior candles in a tree branch with a kindling wood. Each of such candle is handmade and looks incredibly cozy. They are like me, profess Sustainable Design, candles have special variables cartridges sold separately.

Diwali
◉ diwali.ua
🅕 Diwali Candle Shop
Candles made of soy wax in concrete vases of interesting shapes and textures, which can then be perfectly used for small flowers. Brand's hit fragrances are Norwegian Wood in Cinnamon Rolls.

COZINESS CREATORS:

Woolkrafts
🏠 www.woolkrafts.com
◉ woolkrafts
🅕 woolkrafts
Interesting, creative plaids that you want to look at and touch. With beautiful prints and a successful combination of colors. In the designs of the brand there is always something unusual. For example, a plaid with a map of Kiev, a plaid-cactus or a Porto plaid with a landscape of the coast of Portugal. In addition, I am very impressed by the individual approach of the team; they can "revive" the plaids and with the help of personalization make each one very special. With their designs, they prove the theory that plaids should not be boring.

PRIKLADNOE ISKUSSTVO
🏠 www.appliedart.tilda.ws
◉ Prikladnoe_iskusstvo
Objects of modern decorative and applied art from extra fine hypoallergenic Merino Wool. The key to the brand is humanism. On all the stages of production and packaging, they use only those processes and materials that do not harm the environment. All works are limited, with a production of only 15 copies each. Merino is bought on the Lanerossi manufactory, which has been producing yarn since 1817. Each product is attached with a certificate of quality of wool, from which it is made.

Ohaina
🏠 www.ohaina.ua
◉ ohainamyplace
Designer collections of knitted décor, interior items, clothing and exclusive souvenirs. Perfect gifts and non-trivial products for design.

If you're in search of things for coziness, the following places are also worth visiting:
- yasykdeco
- Ба/Льон
- Oshainua

TABLE SETTING:

NEST
🏠 www.nesthomegoods.com
📷 nest.homegoods
f nest.homegoods
✉ Office@nesthomegoods.com

Kitchen textiles of stylish shades and of the best quality. I love and often use their linen tablecloths, napkins and runners in setting the table. This is a basic décor, but for some reason I want to have all the colors and shades.

Some more beautiful decor for table setting can be found here:
- Porshen
- wooden_day
- linewoodua
- Woodstuffhome

POSUDMEISTER
🏠 www.posudmeister.ua
📷 posudmeister

POSUDMEISTER is a place where you can buy the necessary dishes for the preparation and design of any type of table setting. Here everyone will find something to one's taste – from the trivet to the crystal champagne bucket or exquisite collections of porcelain dishes. This is a real paradise for the lovers of high quality and beautiful dishes.

LIGHT:

- lihtar.com.ua
- Svetoria
- Pikart Lights
- Yalanzhi.objects

VASES AND FLOWERS:

Kyivjungles – greening up the house.
Floracontora – flowers for every day. Service "flowers in the house".
Don Pion – the best in service and the kings of punctuality.

MULTIBRAND STORES:

Patte-Patte Baby shop
⌂ patte-patte.com.ua
⊙ pattepatte_baby
Outlet town "Manufactura"
Khodosiyivka village, Berezova, 2, lot 214
Mega cozy children's store that evokes a feeling of tenderness and desire to have a few more children. One wants to watch and buy everything, and there are a lot things to buy – furniture, decorations, goods for kids and mothers, and toys from the world's best manufacturers.

Klovsky garden
⊙ klovsky_sad
Kyiv, Klovsky descent 11

Gallery-shop, floristic store and just a place for filling a soul, the place where the beauty lives. Its feature is the uniqueness of the exhibits: from ebony from Sri Lanka to candlesticks of Ukrainian crafters from Kolomyia – for any budget and wallet. And the most interesting thing is the gallery format: every three months the exposition by themes changes. In general, highly recommend!

Good Wine – Ukrainian analogue of WholeFoods with boutique coffee shops, cozy coffee rooms, own bakery and the home department.

POSTERS:

- colored.phenomena
- lilit_artstore
- olha_stepanian
- mazur_skrobova

PAINTS:

Decoratorskyi
🏠 www.decoratorskyi.com
f decoratorskyi

About the role of colors in my life (but not just that) I have already said enough in this book. My life changed a lot after I discovered them. I like the color palette, their complex, noble shades. At Decoratorskyi, you can also choose the right baseboard, rugs and order a service for sewing and updating furniture.

Barvaland
🏠 www.barvaland.com
📷 barvaland.paint

If you like natural colors and shades or someone in your family suffers from allergy, then choose Barvaland paints. This is the first exclusive collection of ecological paints in Ukraine. And don't be afraid to experiment: everything can be repainted again. Our grandparents not so long ago whitewashed the walls twice a year.

NOW LET'S WALK AROUNDTHE WORLD:

BELGIUM
Baobab www.baobabcollection.com – candles
Atelier\belge www.atelierbelge.eu – beautiful shelves and décor, they plant a tree for each unit of goods sold
Koperhuis www.koperhuis.be – furniture and decorations made of natural materials
Ethnicraft www.ethnicraft.com/international – furniture and accessories
Buzzi Space www.buzzi.space – make almost everything from textile
Gardeco www.gardeco.eu – exclusive sculptures, decor items
Henry Dean www.henrydean.be – vases, glass

SWEDEN
Lintex www.lintex.se – writing boards, mobile boards and wallboards
Eldvarm www.eldvarm.com – everything for fireplaces
Swedish Ninja www.swedishninja.com – "Swedish Ninja" was based on the idea that traditional Scandinavian design can be implemented through unexpected expression
Design House of Stokholm www.designhousestockholm.com – select the ideas of designers for development and production

FRANCE
Ibride www.ibride-design.com – they boldly kick around with animals in furniture and decorations
Roche-bobois www.roche-bobois.com/en-UA – unusual shape and palette of colors of furniture and decorations
Atelier C&S Davoy www.ateliers-csd.com – decor items
MAD et Len www.madetlen.com – fragrances, candles
Tolix www.tolix.com/ – exclusive iron furniture
Polyhedre www.polyhedre.com – ceramics

GERMANY
NEXT www.next.design – light

ENGLAND
Mineheart www.mineheart.com/ – classic in modern variations
Thelermonthupton www.thelermonthupton.com – accessories, details
Rory Dobner www.rorydobner.com – hand-painted dishes

NETHERLANDS
Aquanova www.aquanova.com/ – everything for the bathroom
Houseofhome www.houseofhome.eu/ – interesting decorations from all over the world
Dutchdeluxes www.dutchdeluxes.com/en/ – stylish kitchen details
Moooi www.moooi.com/eu/collection – interesting patterns and colors
HK living www.hkliving.nl – decor
Pols Potten www.polspotten.nl – decor

ITALY
Altreforme www.altreforme.com – unusual design and palette of furniture and decorations, furniture with a wow effect

B Home Interiors www.giobagnara.com – leather accessories
Qeeboo www.qeeboo.com – objects, lamps
Alpicashmere www.alonpi.com – plaids (cashmere)

SPAIN
Nomon www.nomon.es – clocks

PORTUGAL
Anaroque www.ana-roque.com – furniture

DENMARK
101 Copenhagen www.01cph.com – ceramics
AYTM www.aytm.dk/inspiration – furniture and accessories
BROSTE COPENHAGEN www.brostecopenhagen.com – interior items, tableware
Bolia www.bolia.com – more expensive line of Lars Larsen Group, the owner of Jysk

CHEQUE REPUBLIC
SKLO www.sklo.com – glass items by Helena Darbujanova
◉ helena.darbujanova – classics in modern design, variations of feminine furniture made of wood

HONG KONG
Sv casa www.sv-casa.com – home accessories
Wolf www.wolf1834.com – leather boxes for jewelry and watches
Igloo Homeware www.igloohk.com/ – graphic furniture, chairs Miyazaki

CHINA (HONG KONG)
Bentuone bentuone.com – mono-design in terms of materials, use of glass, terrazzo, rocks
X+Q www.xiqiart.com/en/ – sculptures

TAIWAN
Haoshi www.haoshi.com.tw/en – clocks, decor items

ISRAEL
Umasqu www.umasqu.com – modern masks

USA
Assouline www.assouline.com – books, albums, gift editions

TURKEY

Nude Glass www.eu.nudeglass.com – tableware, glass

MOROCCO

Moroccan Bazaar www.moroccanbazaar.com – Moroccan furniture and decorations

ARZEN www.arzen.ma – metal, handwork, any objects

FOR YOUR CONVENIENCE, HERE IS A SELECTION OF RUGS:

Vanessa Barragao www.vanessabarragao.com	ⓘ vanessabarragao_work
cc-tapis www.cc-tapis.com	ⓘ cc_tapis
Nanimarquina www.nanimarquina.com	ⓘ nanimarquina_official
Jason Seife www.jasonseife.com	ⓘ Jasonseife
Rose Pearlman www.rosepearlman.com	ⓘ rosepearlman
Doing goods www.doing-goods.com	ⓘ doinggoods
Allyson Rousseau www.allysonrousseau.com	ⓘ allyrous
lrnce www.lrnce.com	ⓘ lrnce
Kustaa Saksi	ⓘ kustaasaksi
Anthropologie Home	ⓘ anthroliving
Judit Just	ⓘ _jujujust_

Afterword

This book would have made my life much easier if I had known the information contained in it much earlier.

For example, rose bowl for cut flowers and kenzan are things you should learn once to prolong the life of flowers at home.

It also works with other knowledge – it's the little secrets and nuances that can significantly change the appearance of the house and your attitude to it.

Home is your mirror.

Look at it. Look closely. Accept and love now. If you do not accept it, you reject a part of yourself, and your way to the place of strength will end without beginning.

Opportunities come and go, and if you have a habit of noticing these opportunities, you are very likely to live a good life.

Because of the cultural, physical, and mental characteristics of people, making a "home that everyone likes" is a hopeless endeavor. It is better to focus on yourself. You are not a gold coin to be liked by all. Even better – the house and its arrangement can be a filter of entry into your ecosystem. Your home, your rules, your coffee.

Home can cure you from depression, create a context and conditions for personal development, become a reliable anchor and trigger for children's formation…, but this is a separate book. Home is the first association that comes to mind when we talk about family values. Home is the first place we think of when we want care and rest.

Read a poem by Jacques Prevert "How to Make a Portrait of a Bird":

First paint a cage
with an open door,
then paint something pretty,
something simple,
something beautiful,
something useful for the bird.

The whole poem you can read here:

I consider this poem a wonderful allegory – if you want to create your place of strength – you need other ways to create it, otherwise you'll just get a house with furniture.

Another thing is to create a context, favorable conditions and not to hurry. In this simple way your home is "written". We create not an interior, but a context for our rest, development and happiness.

Pour faire le portrait d'un oiseau
Peindre d'abord une cage
avec une porte ouverte
peindre ensuite
quelque chose de joli
quelque chose de simple
quelque chose de beau
quelque chose d'utile
pour l'oiseau

Placer ensuite la toile contre un arbre
dans un jardin
dans un bois
ou dans une forêt
Se cacher derrière l'arbre
sans rien dire
sans bouger....

Parfois l'oiseau arrive vite
mais il peut aussi bien mettre de longues années
avant de se décider
Ne pas se décourager
attendre
attendre s'il le faut pendant des années
la vitesse ou la lenteur de l'arrivée de l'oiseau
n'ayant aucun rapport
avec la réussite du tableau

Quand l'oiseau arrive
s'il arrive
observer le plus profond silence
attendre que l'oiseau entre dans la cage
et quand il est entré
fermer doucement la porte avec le pinceau
puis
effacer un à un tous les barreaux
en ayant soin de ne toucher aucune des plumes de l'oiseau

Faire ensuite le portrait de l'arbre
en choisissant la plus belle de ses branches
pour l'oiseau
peindre aussi le vert feuillage et la fraîcheur du vent
la poussière du soleil
et le bruit des bêtes de l'herbe dans la chaleur de l'été
et puis attendre que l'oiseau se décide à chanter

Si l'oiseau ne chante pas
c'est mauvais signe
signe que le tableau est mauvais
mais s'il chante c'est bon signe
signe que vous pouvez signer

Alors vous arrachez tout doucement
une des plumes de l'oiseau
et vous écrivez votre nom
dans un coin du tableau.

Jacques Prevert

Sometimes "thank you" we perceive as a rule of being a well-mannered person. People stopped to attach a great importance to this word; it has long since lost its huge power: "thank you" here and "thank you" there. Sometimes it is even used as a joke "great thanks (not)".

But I still live with this huge feeling of gratitude. Especially this word – "thank you" – brings me a huge motivation to act.

I do this, looking into a person's eyes and if he or she hides them, I try to take their hand and say: "Just get me correctly. Thank you!"

You may ask how to give thanks well? It would be great if you say the words of gratitude and point out what the person has brought to your life. Try, instead of saying "thank you for bread," to just express your feelings of gratitude for someone's attention and care. Instead of saying "thanks for washing my car," show how important this person is in your life, show love in your actions.

We are grateful to our families for their unconditional support and love, for the opportunity to be the happiest with them.

Give thanks to each other and be grateful to the universe that gives us such an expensive gift as friendship and opportunity to feel and live.

I'm really grateful to

Aliona Severenchuk for teaching me to trust people – I believe without questions, without any agreements; for friendship and my perception of the Ukrainian language.

Maryna Sydorenko for her talent, mutual trust and understanding that talented people are talented in everything. I guess, if you cooked pureed soups or raised chickens that would be the best soups and chickens!

Victoria Prorok for showing how different and alike we are at one time; for my believing that diligence and attentiveness are innate gifts. And for that #wearethesameflock.

Thanks to those who believed in us and our strength and bought this book.

www.ingramcontent.com/pod-product-compliance
Lightning Source LLC
Chambersburg PA
CBHW051332110526
44590CB00032B/4495